Uncle Frank's Guide
To Joining the Workforce

A Companion for Your Job Search

Frank J. Bonsignore

Catawba Street Press

To the late Nelson W. Freeling

For his patient listening, wise counsel, and gentle encouragement.

Introduction

Welcome to the Rat Race! This book is intended for recent college or secondary school graduates who have just entered or will shortly be entering the workforce. My goal is to provide fundamental situational and behavioral knowledge and tactics to "succeed" (whatever that means) at an organization that will be — or perhaps currently is — paying you to show up every day and do something. My starting assumptions are four-fold: First, that you are a mature adult in North America without any work experience except for summer jobs. Second, you don't have any substance abuse problems. Third, you have completed some training beyond secondary school, such as a vocational school, community college or four-year college. Fourth, you have at least average intellect and common sense. Perhaps you might desire to get some work experience before pursuing an advanced degree.

The optimum time for you to begin reading this book is the summer *before* your last year in school. But better late than never.

Who am I? As you read this book, you will learn more about me. For now, think of me as your Uncle Frank.

Most people would agree that a person learns things as they rack up time in the working world. Some refer to them as Life Lessons. I'm sharing mine—in a conversational style—to help you to avoid behavior in the early stages of your career that can impede your advancement. By the way, I view a career as a job you want to stay at to learn and gain experience.

Years ago, when I was entering the workforce, the frequency of people changing jobs was not as high as it appears to be today. Of course, there were not the large-scale layoffs that are so commonplace now, so there was a greater sense of loyalty to a company. Once you were hired by Fabulous Flanges, Inc., (a mythical company that I invented to stage some of my advice instead of saying 'ABC Company') if you didn't cause any trouble, worked hard, and weren't too obvious a goof-off, you could be a "lifer" there—start after college, spend the next forty years working there while you married and had children and grandchildren, and then retire and collect a generous pension. Today, that's not the way it is, for so many reasons beyond your control. I can say only two things with any certainty: 1) there are many reasons that the job market has changed and 2) everybody *thinks* they know why. I won't bore you with my thoughts on that topic, but will, however, let you benefit from my experience in working with and keenly observing people in the world of work for more than twenty-five years. No, I haven't seen it all, but I have seen enough to pass on some helpful information to you. I've made my share of mistakes but have also been intelligent enough to learn from most of them.

What you're reading might be called a summary of things to do and things to avoid doing from the perspective of an uncle speaking to his nephews and nieces. Why from an uncle? Well, I think that advice received from an uncle is somewhat more palatable than that from a parent, and more easily considered as a possible course of action by someone such as yourself, who is becoming increasingly independent from his parents. The wise, helpful uncle has the concern, but without the strong emotional involvement that a parent has, because he doesn't share the responsibility for you being on this earth. At the same time he gives no-nonsense advice. He is objective, non-judgmental, and has a good idea what the working world is like. When I left for college many years ago, *my* Uncle Pete gave me a piece of paper with some sage advice and twenty dollars: "Dear Frank: Always remember: Mouth shut, bowels open, always ask for a receipt. Good luck. Pete." If you think about it, that is pretty good overall advice, but I'm going to delve deeper on a wider range of issues based on my experience. I'll also be telling you about some incidents that I or a colleague/friend/acquaintance did not handle correctly, and the subsequent lessons to learn. When I tell you about experiences I had at work, it's not to garner sympathy; I only want to share the lesson. As you accrue time in the world of work, you'll have your own stories to tell.

You're not going to be reading profound wisdom; it's pretty much common sense with a dash of cynicism because I'm a smart-aleck. It's the truth as I know it, and simple to comprehend. Of course, you will have to adapt what you read to your particular situation. I've also written this from a technical person's perspective because that's my background, but I believe that the basic principles I'm selling (and start believing *right now* with all your heart that work and life from this day forward are *always* about selling) are applicable to just about anyone. Another concept to remember is that no one, in any job, is indispensable.

Along the way to writing this book, I've found quotes that condense important topics to their essence. Think about these quotes; they can help you develop your own thoughts, questions, and insights on various aspects and situations of the workplace.

Enjoy the cartoons I've chosen for you, but think about what the take-away message is.

So. . . let's get to work!

Chapter 1
Getting Started

For the first time in many years, you have no homework, no exams to study for, no papers to write, and you are relieved. Here's a bracing thought: Everything else was preparatory; now the real work begins!

In the United States and Canada, and probably elsewhere, everyone has the *right to an education, the right to apply for work wherever you want and the right to not be discriminated against for your beliefs, race,* et cetera, in the hiring selection process. You are entitled to resign from any job whenever you wish. In many states, companies have the right to employ you *at will,* which means that they can dismiss you for virtually any reason except for the aforementioned examples of discrimination.

Employment is best described as *quid pro quo*—"this for that"—you work, they pay you. You don't work, they fire you. They treat you poorly, you fire *them.*

It's not an exaggeration to say a job search is a multi-million-dollar decision! Multiply the number of years you envision working by the annual salary you expect to earn. Pretty big number, isn't it?

Like any big decision, there are many variables. The seemingly simple task of finding and starting a job has many interrelated decisions. First off, you have to know what you want to do.

Mark Twain said "I can teach anybody how to get what they want out of life. The problem is that I can't find anybody who can tell me what they want." I'll begin with the working assumption that you are in your final year, or have completed a course of study, at a college (or even a secondary school) that trained you to do something or work in a specific field.

A reasonable first step is to research companies or organizations that hire people with the skills you will have after graduation. That seemingly simple task has another level such as your preferred location. Open to North America? Wonderful! Your options will be greater than someone who wants a specific city.

How about the size of the organization? Want to teach in a public or private school? Located where—in a urban or rural area? What about size? Big school district? Desire to be an engineer at a company with 50,000 employees or one with 5,000? Or 500? Or 5? Does a company that is multi-national appeal to you over one that is pretty much domestic? Do you want a private company or one that is publicly traded? Perhaps you don't care much about the company as long as you get to work at what you want to do? And money: how much do jobs in your field pay?

I don't think you need to have *all* the answers to *all* of the questions right now, but they will come up as your job search progresses.

If you don't know what companies to start looking at, the

professors at your school can help guide and advise you. Better yet, they may know someone in an organization that is doing what you are interested in. But you have to put in some thinking first. You don't want to pose the question "Know any companies I can apply to?" With that approach, they might recommend the fast-food restaurant down the street. Ask to meet with them during their scheduled office hours for advisement. When you do meet, approach them in this fashion to get some guidance or tap into their psyches:

"Professor Cranium, I'm beginning to look at organizations that may hire me after graduation. In the class I had with you last semester, you referred to some of your experiences when you were employed at Fabulous Flanges. Would you tell me more about that?"

From that point, the conversation can go anywhere. Your professor may tell you his personal story or even turn the question back to you: "What do you envision doing after graduation?" You should do some thinking up front and will leave the meeting with additional things to consider. This will help you in conjunction with your own research. From the discussion you have with him, you can further research those organizations and follow up with him to share what you found and thank him for his guidance.

Another valuable resource is the placement office at your school. Besides being responsible for coordinating visits from hiring organizations to interview graduating students, they will most likely have information and coaching on writing resumes and cover letters, interviewing, and career fairs, all of which I discuss later in this chapter. I suggest that you take advantage of the many services the placement office offers—you paid for it with your tuition dollars.

As you begin the process of job searching, there are three important ideas to remember:

First, realize that you *will likely* have to make some compromises. For example, a job you like may be a long commute from your residence. The company may have a strict dress code or be located in an area where there aren't many social activities or which has extremes in temperature. Expecting to get everything can be disappointing, but you should definitely try. If you do get exactly what you want, thank the Almighty and have fun. Enjoy that ride.

Second, decide what's acceptable and unacceptable to you. Perhaps it's a must-have that the company encourages continuing education, or requires minimal or extensive travel, or international sales.

Third (and this can be challenging), when you interview, pay close attention to what you're seeing and hearing. You need to get an accurate picture of the daily aspects of the job. I've always found that it's all a big blur during the interview. I'm going to talk much more about interviews later, but for now, realize that sometimes what you see and hear as a candidate might not be what you get as an employee. It's strange if you think about it: you interview with a company for a couple hours, maybe returning for a second or third interview and from those minimal encounters, you and the employer each make a decision.

It's unfortunate that you can't "date" for a while before you decide. This is all the more reason to do as much research as possible on a company and be very observant and *know what you want* when you interview. Include *everything*—your future boss, colleagues, location of the company and how clean the work areas are kept—in your observations. It is a lot like sizing up the qualities of a potential life partner. Some things you have to leave to chance and figure them out along the way.

Your transition into the world of work is a major change in your life. People will see you in a different light and, right or wrong, have expectations of you. Your parents might be looking for you to become independent from them and be a fine, upstanding productive, taxpaying citizen. Perhaps you and your girl or boyfriend have spoken of marriage, and of course getting a job is the logical next step. Your student loan creditors might also be anxious for you to start repaying them. And you are probably more than ready to leave the frugal life of a student, begin earning a salary, and start living your adult life. With this in mind, you should know the salary range for the type of job you are seeking.

Here is a must-have:

Be comfortable and happy with the specific job YOU accept. The choice of how you make your living and what job you pursue has to come from YOU, not your parents, not your fiancé, not your friends. They may point out positive and negative aspects of the job that you may have overlooked and, yes, you should pay attention to these things and give them some thought. But YOU are the one who has to show up every day and do the work. And it is not worth it if you're not going to be comfortable.

Anyone, including me, will tell you that no job is without its difficulties, boredom, and unpleasant periods, and that no one starts out at the top. But if you couple that with discontent, a general blah feeling, and an absence of passion and purpose, the road can be rough.

What if your degree doesn't match directly to a career?

There are a variety of vehicles for figuring out what career matches your skills and interests. And the amount of effort you expend will directly correlate with your level of job satisfaction. Begin by getting a copy of the book *What Color is Your Parachute?* by Richard N. Bolles, and reserve some time to read and complete the exercises he supplies. The book has many thought-provoking tasks for you to complete if you want to get the most out of the book. Do not skip them if they seem too time-consuming, or feel that you can work it out in your head and not write it down. The act of writing helps you by feeding back to your brain when you re-read what you previously wrote. You think—you write—you see and read—and you think some more. When what you write down doesn't make sense, or if you struggle to put it into words, it should send up a flag that this area might require more effort.

If you need more help, or perhaps a different type of help, there are resources such as psychological tests, consultants, therapists, or people sometimes referred to as *coaches*. If they are qualified, some of these people can administer tests and help with the interpretation of the results. But remember: *The answer is within you. The tests are there to help coax the answer from you.*

I read somewhere that the definition of a consultant is ". . . someone who borrows your watch to tell you what time it is." And it's true—any type of facilitator, be he a coach or degreed shrink, sees or hears aspects of yourself that you may not be aware of—and points it out to you or brings it up for discussion. Getting help from someone is not something to be ashamed of. You are asking for guidance to the answer, not the answer itself, however appealing the latter may seem.

If you are considering a coach, be aware that they aren't *necessarily* psychologists and aren't *necessarily* trained. I think the credentials for the field of coaching are evolving. Here are some guidelines:

- Have a brief initial telephone conversation during which you ask about their credentials or resume. Inquire from what walks of life their clients come from, how long they have been in that business, and if they have any industrial experience.

- Avoid someone who suddenly decides he wants to coach other people and feels he's qualified because he ". . . likes talking to people." Listen to your gut feeling about this person. Get a perspective of what he has accomplished in his life.

- Anyone can give you an opinion, but what you want is *direction* on moving forward towards a career.
- Very important is the issue of money. Alarms should go off if you are asked for a sum of money up front.
- Run fast from anyone who *guarantees* they can help you. They should only agree to work with you. If you read an advertisement or view an infomercial that says: "Success for only $199.95! Get the complete set of DVD's *to transform your life!*" the best thing to do is STOP!

It is fair to say that most people, at one time or another, may feel uncertainty in their life and spend some time soul-searching and wondering about opportunities they didn't pursue. If, during a reflective time, you come upon an extremely fluent person advertising a program that can part the clouds and show you the path to finding success in your life, earning enormous amounts of money, and achieving unlimited potential, it's difficult to squelch your curiosity. The information you are offered generally takes the form of books and recorded visual media or even seminars where the principal or one of his/her disciples will present the tenets of their program. You will see testimony from people who have completed the course and have achieved everything they dreamed. He will be interviewed on board his 50-foot yacht or in an expansive house in a sunny climate or island paradise. They have sparkling white smiles and if they're Caucasian, a nice tan. Their significant others are amazingly gorgeous. The program will not be inexpensive but they stress that the value you will get from achieving wealth and advancement will outweigh the funds you have to supply now. "Isn't *your success* worth it?" is a popular phrase.

Think long and hard before you shell out any money, *especially* if there is a limited time offer. While I have not invested in any programs of this nature (other than a single book) I have examined many of them with a critical but objective eye, and as you might guess, I'm not impressed. The issue I have is that these people who have achieved tremendous wealth and want to sell their plan to you *haven't done anything!* None of them ever account for some period of time in the working world, but they all seem to say that they were, at one point in their lives, dirt poor and frustrated that they couldn't achieve their goals. They had no money, were homeless, and . . . blah blah blah, then I discovered how to think and become rich!" Well, they're not totally off base: becoming wealthy does involve *a lot* of thinking but it involves much more *doing*.

My itch with these programs is that their creators offer one-size-fits-all blueprints for not a small amount of cash *while the answers you get come from within you.* And yes, no matter whom you consult with, the information that will eventually guide someone to help you will come from you. Nevertheless, these people became wealthy by carefully putting together their spiel and selling it to you. No reputable, ethical coach or counselor that you would see on a one-to-one or group basis would claim that they have a method that unleashes unlimited potential in you.

The counterargument that these pitchmen might offer is that several sessions with a consultant may cost more than their introductory program, ". . .which is *proven* to work!" They might argue that after all, coaches need to eat too, so isn't in their best interest to keep you coming back? They put any kind of spin on their program to make it sound appealing.

So if you decide to go the route of individual career counseling, go in with an agenda and agree with your provider on an action plan with a date or number of visits at which you can recap, review what you have learned, and decide if you want to continue. Your college placement office is good place to begin your search or get recommendations for a career coach. You can also Google "career coaches" and your city and state location to find people in that field.

Introducing LinkedIn (www.linkedin.com)

The world of work revolves around people. And people, whether they be colleagues, relatives, fellow students, friends — are *contacts*. You already have plenty of contacts — your friends over the years, your relatives, and bosses from your summer jobs, internships, or co-ops. You may call these people when you need help or need to know something. In the business world, they are the people who help you do your job — it's all about teamwork. So for example, if during the course of your job you have to ship something to a foreign trade zone, there is, not surprisingly, paperwork that has to be completed and it has to be done correctly or your important item is left on a shipping dock someplace far from where you intended it to be. You will probably have a contact who not only knows how to do that, it could be their occupation. Another example: you purchase some circuit boards and the company doubles your order. You receive the boards, put them to use, and a few weeks later get a call from your vendor, asking for either the extra boards to be shipped back or another purchase order for them. Your contact (actually *my contact* — this actually happened to me) in purchasing took care of the problem. You will be somebody else's contact — you will make someone else breathe a sigh of relief when you make a problem go away or help them in some fashion.

With a LinkedIn account (a basic membership is free), you connect with the people in many aspects of your world — business, personal, and educational. Once you connect with someone, you can view *each other's* contacts. You can ask your contact for an introduction to one of their contacts who has a profile that interests you. After being introduced, you can arrange to meet the other person to discuss their career or whatever facet caught your interest. I do not think the developers wanted it to be used as a dating site. You can also do research on companies and find out the *names of people who work there* and see if you are connected to anyone who is connected to them. You can also locate companies by business type, geographic location, number of employees and get the URL for their website. It's a very useful tool to help you identify and locate companies where you might want to work and people who may be able to help you get there. Begin by connecting with people you know: professors, friends of your family, relatives, your colleagues from previous jobs, friends, fellow students, and anyone else with whom you have become acquainted or have admiration and respect.

LinkedIn is a form of social networking, but not in the same way as Facebook. It focuses on business and career contacts, documents your experience and who you are connected to, shows your goals, and lists opportunities that you might want to pursue. You can share what you want and it's evergreen, so that you can highlight experience or transfers from one job to the next. Recruiters too use LinkedIn as a resource for locating candidates for open positions.

- Being a newcomer to the world of work, your profile on LinkedIn may be brief. After all, you're just starting out, so how much information can you be expected to have? It's quality rather than quantity. Start with your career goal:

  "I'm interested in a marketing-sales position where I can work with people on the technical aspects of a product."

  "My interests lie in the field of forensic accounting. I have strong analytical skills and love numerical puzzles."

  "Biomedical engineering is a field where I can provide innovative solutions to medical problems."

You should include:

- What school you attended, when you expect to receive your degree and in what field
- Specialized coursework
- Internships
- Research or work you have done with or for your professors

- Computer expertise or even something like "Proficient with Microsoft Office, Linux, Ubuntu, and Mac operating systems."
- Valuable skills you have *with examples to illustrate their authenticity*. It's fine to include examples such as serving on the student council or a school organization that may have helped you develop or demonstrate your teamwork and leadership abilities.

Most importantly, LinkedIn can help you connect with people who work in the area you want to work in or are interested in. You can also sort this information according to their location, which enables you to see whom you might be able to connect with. LinkedIn allows people to share as much or as little of their professional lives as they wish. Some profiles are very brief without any specifics or contact details, while others are quite extensive.

In terms of connecting with other individuals on LinkedIn, the protocol varies from person to person.

Some people connect only with people they have met and "know" while others will connect with someone who has only asked them to connect and explained why they want to. You should refrain from saying that you want to add someone ". . . to your professional network." Include some additional explanation: *"In spring of this year I expect to receive my degree in Electrical Engineering from your alma mater and am interested in working in the field in which you have experience: control systems and algorithms. I would like to add you to my network on LinkedIn as a resource for advice and direction as I pursue my career."* Or something to that effect. There is a limit to the number of characters you can have in an invitation to connect, so you will have to choose your words carefully.

As you increase the number of your connections, you will see people in your network who are connected to people with whom you'd like to connect. LinkedIn has the utility for you to ask people to introduce you to others to whom they are connected. Having someone to grease the skids for you always helps.

And just for the record, I have a profile on LinkedIn and I have not received any payment from them to promote their site.

It doesn't end with LinkedIn. You should use any resource you discover to help you in your job search. It is perfectly reasonable to share your job search with your friends on Facebook. It's not just what your friends point you towards, but *their* friends, some of whom may be located in a city or industry that you are interested in. For example, posting to your timeline "Hello friends! After graduation from Whatsamatta U. in May with my B.S. in Finance, I am interested in settling in the southwest US. If you know of any opportunities in finance or know people who live in that area, please connect me with them!" If you belong to Toastmasters, a church group, a civic organization like the Rotary or Lions Club or a fraternity, tell them what you are seeking.

The many search engines such as Indeed, Monster, and Google ("zoology jobs in New Mexico") are all useful resources. Some locales distribute free newspapers devoted to job seekers.

Generating contacts

Once you land at a company, generating contacts will become easier. You'll be meeting new people every day. In the meantime, seize opportunities to meet people. For example, volunteering at your school's alumni weekend is a way to meet people to connect with or at least network with. Networking is also known as schmoozing (covered in a later chapter) and is most like fishing on a quiet pond. With a rod and reel, that is, not with a stick of dynamite. If, while handing out cups of punch at the alumni event, an attendee becomes chatty with you, you can casually inquire where they are from and perhaps, as the evening progresses, what their field of study was, gradually finding out where their line of work. It's more like you're a cat rubbing against their ankle and hoping they'll reach down and pet you as opposed to a pit-bull's amorous intents on your leg. Think smooth and slow.

Use your discretion; not every situation or social event should be viewed as a pool of possible contacts. Funerals, no; weddings, fine, but only during the reception, not while the bride and groom are exchanging vows.

It's helpful to be creative in your search to connect with people in your desired career. Though I have not attempted this, I can suggest that if you were interested in, for example, financial planning, attending an open house at a brokerage might be a way to meet and connect with people in that field. Just to be clear, not with people who are deciding to invest their dollars, but the company sponsoring the event. The few that I've attended (to find a financial advisor) had a bunch of well-dressed, friendly people greeting attendees and handing out refreshments. They are trying to sell the idea that they will be helpful in investing your 401-k and pension dollars. If you attend, neatly dressed, and explain to those in charge that you're interested in exploring the field of financial advisement and just want to sit quietly and observe, I can't vouch for what they might say, but it would not be unreasonable for them to welcome you. You could probably stay afterwards to connect with the people sponsoring the event and ask them any questions you may have and inquire about what qualities they expect in a candidate. Similarly, you could seek out local engineering societies, human resource networks, or other professional organizations in your field. You don't necessarily have to become a dues-paying member, and any connections you make could be valuable. If you can speak to a representative of the organization prior to the meeting, introduce yourself as a student or recent graduate and ask to attend the next meeting. It is likely they will be interested in a potential new member. Ask how people dress for the event—business casual, or sport coat and tie for men and perhaps slacks with a conservative blouse and blazer for women. Then show up and *be prepared to speak clearly and concisely about yourself and your goals*. You will also have the opportunity to ask the attendees about themselves.

My intent here has been to encourage you to think creatively about meeting people and networking, to make connections that in turn will aid you in locating and possibly interviewing for a position in your field. Now we have to talk about cover letters, resumes and job interviews.

Chapter 2
Two Essential Documents

This cartoon pokes fun at nepotism. The young man is the nephew of Cora, who is Mr. Dithers' wife. *This happens all the time.*

The first image potential employers will have of you will be your cover letter and resume, which I've always felt are two of the most painful but critical documents to create. When you are responding to a posted job opening (some places have "job boards" with active openings posted on an actual or electronic bulletin board), you write a cover letter to introduce yourself to the hiring manager, HR person, or individual receiving responses for the position. This document specifies what job you are applying for, why you feel you are qualified for the job and why you want it. There is a plethora of opinions on what to include, how to phrase it, and how to format it. Its criticality stems from the decision a potential employer makes when it's viewed—if *he/she even read it.* I've heard stories where the first thing recruiters do is rip the cover letter off, and other anecdotes where they use them as a screening tool. You have no control over how they are handled but there are some hard and fast rules for resumes and cover letters that I want to mention.

Grammar and spelling should be perfect. No excuses. Have a friend proofread your cover letter and resume, even if you have spell-checked it numerous times. If no one is around, read it aloud as you point to each word.

Illustrate the skills you used in your previous jobs, as meager as they may be. But don't be ridiculous: If you mowed lawns in the summer, drove the truck and directed the crew, don't pump it up as a "Personnel and Transportation Manager of Botanical Growth Technicians." Say "Crew chief responsible for two trucks and four team members." Everybody sees through over-the-top embellishment. Do not neglect mentioning your accomplishments. If your friendly attitude to neighboring homeowners resulted in additional business by all means mention it: "Increased residential business by 25% over previous years." During an interview, you might be asked how you accomplished that: "I developed a brochure and left one at each of the houses adjacent to those we serviced, and told the homeowners that I would be delighted to earn their business. My crew and I were always friendly and courteous to any passers-by, and we left each house clear of all clippings and debris."

- You are not applying to be a boy or girl scout. Don't list attributes such as "trustworthy and hardworking, with customer focus and dedication to task", "conscientious, detail-oriented, reliable, independent self-starter". Employers expect that you have all those attributes. Your employer will be the first to tell you during your exit interview if you aren't focused on the task and are not reliable and trustworthy, Besides, would any sane person admit he is dishonest and unmotivated?

- Cover letters should be concise and tell the recipient who you are and what area or job you're interested in. If you can find recent news about the company, mention it: *"I'm submitting my resume for the position of marketing coordinator at Fabulous Flanges. The growth your company has attained is impressive. A recent article in Useful Metal Products said*

Fabulous Flanges is well known for their comprehensive product line, and projects sales this year will increase by 50%. I would like to be part of a growing company with a product line applicable to a wide industrial segment."

- Tell them why they should consider you for a position. Here is where you place your long-standing interest and preferably experience in the job area or your interest in working for the company: *"I worked summers during college on the Hot Springs geothermal station in downstate New York. The safety of our crew depended on the quality of your products."*

- Thank the recipient for their (anticipated) consideration of you for employment. Mention your intended follow-up: a phone call in the next week, an email, or you can even suggest a one-on-one meeting: *"Thank you for considering me as a candidate for this position. I look forward to hearing from you." OR "I would appreciate the opportunity to meet with you to discuss my credentials and your requirements for candidate employees in your marketing department."*

- If you are going to snail-mail your cover letter and resume, don't try and make a hard copy of your resume stand out from those of other candidates by printing it on light blue or off-white paper. Make sure that both the paper and the printer are of higher quality. Stick with a standard font, like 12pt. Times New Roman, not Comic Sans or anything fancy.

- Creating your resume can be frustrating because everyone has an opinion on them. You won't please everyone, but you should get comments on your resume from career counselors at your school, from recruiters, (most often referred to as headhunters) or people working in your desired field.

- Tailor your resume to the job. Everybody hates to hear this because of the pain and suffering they experienced writing the first one. Tweak your resume to the job so that it highlights any relevant skills. Although the jobs you apply for may have a common thread, the company and the industry will change. Suppose you are especially environmentally conscious, worked a summer job maintaining parks and beaches, and are a member of the Sierra Club. If you are applying for an accountant position at a company that markets water pollution control products, you may want to highlight your relevant experience. You are essentially saying *"See, I think like you do. So why not hire me?"*

Believe me, though, all this is a lot easier with a computer. Ask your grandparents about something called a typewriter.

Chapter 3
Finding a Place to Land

Sometimes a job opening can be right under your nose.

Classified job postings

Announcements for jobs are classified by the field or job category, though there is a category called General Labor for jobs that do not require specific training other than excellent attendance and a strong work ethic, which, by the way, are essential for *any* job.

For virtually any city, state, province, village, town, hamlet, et cetera, on planet Earth, Craigslist has a page that contains everything from classified listings of jobs, things for sale, and many other categories. The jobs category can contain scam listings and announcements that do not list a company ("blind" listings), so use caution. Nevertheless, legitimate job opportunities are announced there.

Indeed.com is an excellent site that is used by many other job-sourcing sites. You specify what you are looking for and what location of the city, country or world. It helps you make your search as specific as possible. For example, if you enter "marketing" in the "what" field, it will immediately list subcategories such as marketing manager, marketing coordinator, marketing research, marketing specialist, and so on.

A third site is Monster.com, a popular job posting board with many options. After signing up for a free account, you can have several different resumes stored to use for different jobs. You can also make your resume available for employers and employment agencies (headhunters) to view.

By now you should also have a profile on LinkedIn. Even though you do not know someone, you can, if you feel bold enough, send them an invitation to connect. LinkedIn recommends that you connect only to people you know (or at least have met or spoken to) but there are people who have an "open" network, where they connect with anyone who invites them. I maintain an open but selective network. When invited to connect to someone I do not know, I will decide to accept their invitation by seeing what common connections we have. Because I'm a technical person, I decline invitations to connect with people not in any of my fields of interest. I wish that LinkedIn had a utility that enabled you to ask someone *why* they invited you to connect. If they want to connect because they know my cousin or think I'm handsome, I probably won't accept (though I might be flattered). I think it's best to keep a LinkedIn profile for professional connections. Facebook is there for social connections.

There are usually free tabloids dedicated to people who are looking for a job. They are worth examining because even if you do not find jobs in your field, you may get ideas of companies to research that may employ people with your qualifications.

Connected to the State Department of Labor are agencies to assist job seekers. Sources and websites that these agencies use in their searches may overlap those you use, but their offices and counselors are an excellent asset. They are not a "stop in and visit" agency. You will probably have to register and fill out some application, but the time can be worth the effort.

Counties and towns usually have their own websites which include lists of job vacancies. Civil service jobs may require passing a test and achieving a high ranking on a roster of candidates. The tests for these positions are scheduled and announced, so if you're interested you should request an email notification. Some civil service positions require the employee to reside in the town of employment.

Campus recruiters and job fairs

As a student, your first interview might be with a recruiter visiting your school. Companies will request permission to hold interviews at schools noted for the quality of their graduates. Don't rely only on your school for interviews, as there are other venues such as job fairs which might also be held at your school or in the neighboring community. Job fairs are a hubbub of activity, like a county fair but without pony rides for the children and rigged-for-your-loss games of chance. A list of the companies that plan on attending will be published so that you can target specific companies and research them beforehand.

If you get to a job fair too early, some of the companies may not be ready to interview, but by getting there too late you risk standing in lines that may be quite lengthy. Some companies (Apple, Microsoft, PlayStation, etc.) are magnets for new talent. From my experience, it's best to show up about ten minutes before the posted start time. By arriving early, you might be able to scout out where the companies you want to visit are located in the room and plan your attack.

Because the representatives from the companies may have limited time to spend with you, it is crucial that you impress them or make them remember you over the many other eager faces they will see. At the end of the day, they may have a thick stack of resumes but all you care about is the one with your name on it.

One technique that may help a recruiter remember you is to know beforehand what type of position you are seeking, and most importantly, be able to convince the recruiter that you can be of value to the company. This comes with more preparation on your part of what is sometimes referred to as an *elevator speech*, which is a concise statement of *you and the skills you are selling*. Supposedly it's brief enough to say during an elevator ride with someone who has the power to influence your career. For example (and please note that I made up this entire dialog):

"Good morning, my name is Oscar Bassett, and I will be graduating in May from Whatsamatta U with a degree in mechanical engineering and a minor in material science."

[The recruiter will introduce him/herself and ask you what you are interested in. Repeat his name back to him and make sure that you can spell it. If it's a complicated one, ask him/her to write it down or ask for a business card as your conversation is nearing the end.]

You continue with *"From your website I see that Fabulous Flanges has along-standing reputation as the preferred pipefitting supplier for many geothermal companies. I am interested in environmentally friendly technologies like geothermal. My last two co-op positions were with your direct competitor, Fantastic Flanges. They are a fine company, but they focus their efforts on oil platforms which, while profitable for them, isn't in line with my aspirations."*

[Mr. Recruiter will now ask about your specific goals and/or what you worked on at Fantastic Flanges.]

A response could be *"I was involved with correlating metal composition with flange failure at high temperature and pressure applications. This is directly applicable to your geothermal business."*

[Recruiter nods intelligently and pretends to understand what you just said. And perhaps he is impressed with the preparation and research you have done on the company.]

Ask *"Will you be scheduling interviews for candidates with my degree?"*

[Recruiter says that Mr. Department Head will be reviewing resumes and will be contacting candidates they are interested in speaking with. *Try to remember the name of the department head.*]

Keep the connection going: *"I would like to follow up with you. May I have your business card?"* Even if you don't get a business card, following up with the recruiter is still possible, as you do have his name. If you don't get his name, ask at the placement office who the representative was. It might also be in the program for the job fair.

As you told the recruiter, follow up with an email or phone call *the next day*. Mention that you met him at your school and that you are following up with him to schedule a future interview. You might ask for the name of the hiring manager; you may not obtain that information but if you don't ask, you won't get it.

The above scenario serves to give you an *idea* of an encounter with a recruiter. Like many other things, "Your results may be substantially different." Preparation, though, is a key element to achieve a positive outcome.

Consider using business cards to supplement your resume. I've heard these referred to as pocket resumes. You include your name, email, LinkedIn profile address, cell phone number, field of study, your outstanding GPA, and so forth. It's a take-away item, and while the recipient may only shove it into a coat pocket and find it when he wears that outfit again, it's an easy item to supply and can be worthwhile. Perhaps it will be passed to someone else who may be interested in your skills. You can purchase blank stock sold for that purpose—the cards are easily separated without perforations—and print them yourself, or for about twenty dollars you can have five hundred cards printed professionally at Vistaprint.

A company representative at a job fair may not even accept a resume, but tell each person to apply via the company website.

They are there to answer questions about their current openings and the company.

The hidden job market

It's referred to as hidden because there generally aren't any announced openings because you create them. Here's a very general description of an approach that you can build on and adapt to your personal situation:

- You become aware that Fabulous Flanges recently acquired another company or that they have announced an expansion of some sort. Your career goal is in advertising and communications. You know of the company and think it would be a good place to be employed. You also have a LinkedIn account and have been generating contacts by seeing who you might know at the company or who you know that knows someone there. Preferably you have a name and an email or address of someone in the department that is your target. If you can't get a contact, you can consider asking your professors if they know someone there. If that doesn't work, consider asking someone in the placement office at your school. As a last-ditch effort, you can contact HR at the company.

- In a note to your contact at Fabulous Flanges, you offer congratulations on the company's acquisition and remark *"… investing in the gasket product line will foster and broaden your presence in many industries and give you an edge over their competition in the flange industry"* or something to that effect.

- Introduce yourself as a recent college graduate with a major in (Communications, Materials Science, or whatever) who has *"… interest in working in sales geared toward flange products and gaskets"* or something that is specific to you.

- *Ask for advice.* You can even state that you're not going to ask your contact for a job or try and sell him/her something. Say it directly: *"I'm not going to ask you for a job; your advice is what I'm after."* All you want, as a soon-to-be-graduate, is *advice* on how to use your skills to be employed in that particular industry, or who they might know that may be able to help you. You don't include a resume because that implies what? A job! And all you want is advice. Everybody likes to give advice, especially to a young, ambitious, recent or soon-to-be graduate. Well, not everybody. There are some people that act like the male offspring of female canines.

Attach a career or marketing plan to your note. You are marketing *you*, in case you're wondering. A marketing plan is a one-page document that has:

- Your contact information
- A brief statement of your objective "Advertising and sales in industries serving pipefitting applications in extreme environments" You can also include your short- and long-range plans "Project manager within five years, department head after ten years."
- A list of five or six of your main skills and if possible, how you want to use them "competitive and energetic; prefer a fast-paced environment", "creative with innovative ideas", "foster team building and cooperation", "excellent writing and presentation skills". Be prepared to give clear, concrete examples of these skills if asked. If you're fresh out of school, use examples from any of your extracurricular activities or organizations.
- A list of all or many of the companies you are targeting, including the one you are directing the letter to in addition to their competitors.

- Close the letter by thanking the addressee for his/her time. Mention that you can be contacted at your cell number, that you look forward to hearing from them, and close the letter.

The marketing plan document serves to go deeper into who you are and what you want without screaming "Here's my resume! Hire me!" Naturally if you get to speak with someone you can delve deeper into what specific qualifications they look for or what their training consists. You must ask them "Who else can I speak to about my career plans?" to get names of other people to connect with. You should also take advantage of the meeting: "I have to ask, before we end this conversation, are there are any opportunities in your organization for someone with my goals?" You're not tricking them into speaking with you or considering you as a candidate— you genuinely asked them for advice. Besides, put yourself in their position: an ambitious young person comes asking for advice about the industry you currently work in and who he/she can speak with—but does not ask you about possibilities at your company. They might think "What am I—chopped liver?" This is why you include a list of the companies you are targeting—they may know someone at one of them or the list might trigger them to recommend a company you have not included. Of course you have a copy of your actual resume which you leave with them to perhaps forward to someone who is hiring.

All of these activities can be difficult, but the alternative is for someone from Human Resources to send out a note thanking you for your interest in their company and if you submit a resume, they'll keep it on file for future openings. Going through HR is, in my opinion and experience, a waste of time since they respond to "official" (generated by departments within the company) requests for additional personnel.

Chapter 4
The Interview and Beyond

What employers want

While only "they" know for sure, let's talk about some positive characteristics that are desirable in the workplace.

Employers like to see confident, intelligent, well-mannered individuals that are eager to learn, dedicated to the job, reliable, honest, and serious about their career.

Confidence: A confident person knows the boundaries of their knowledge of a subject. They tell the truth without embellishment. Some may say they are factual but humble. People easily approach them. They are not arrogant.

Intelligence: Perhaps one way is knowing usage of *your, you're, there, their,* and *they're.* No matter how picayune it may appear, my opinion of an adult native speaker of the English language is tarnished when they err using those words. Many but not all intelligent people have *common sense,* which is knowledge about interacting with others and handling everyday situations. It is also called *good judgment.* Be aware, though, as one colleague of mine told me "Good judgment comes from experience. Experience comes from bad judgment." Learning from your mistakes is one way of increasing your intelligence in that you know how to react to a situation.

Well-mannered: People with manners are polite, use the words *please* and *thank you* and are not unusually loud and boisterous or chew with their mouths open. Look for the person who is called a lady or gentleman.

Eager to learn: Your job is actually the next phase of your education, so you should understand that you do not know everything about your chosen field. Realizing that you don't know everything will convey through your words and actions that you are, in fact, eager to learn.

Dedication to the job: Our lives have many dimensions of which work is anessential one. To have dedication to your job means that while you are at work, you have diligence and focus on what is expected of you. Other aspects of your life will come to mind while you are at work, but try to keep those issues from dominating your thoughts. It would be ridiculous to expect concerns about an ill relative, a new romantic interest, or a pending vacation not to enter your mind, but arrive at work on time, get your work done, and don't be the first one out the door when the workday ends.

Reliable: Barring illness or personal catastrophe, you should show up every day. Second, you should deliver assigned projects in the time frame which was agreed upon. If you are going to be late with your deliverables, tell your boss *before* you are late, explain why, and make sure it is the absolute truth. Good reasons for being late? *"I underestimated the time required to complete the task,"* or *"I became confused with one part of the project. I needed clarification which put me behind schedule."*

Honest: This also includes truthfulness and transparency among people you work with. Don't intentionally deceive *anyone* or be devious with your colleagues.

Serious about your career: This is almost redundant; the previous attributes will indicate that you value your job and want to do it well.

Before you shake your head in disbelief about my words, realize that no one exhibits these traits all of the time. There are no perfect employees.

The interview

I've heard from many people that it's during the first few minutes of an interview that a manager or representative from a company decides if you are an acceptable candidate. You have to send out the right signals, and since the first thing the interviewer sees is *you,* your personal image is just as important as your image on paper. Regarding dressing for an interview:

- For many positions, conservative dress is appropriate. For men, this translates to a darker color sport coat or blazer with a white or light blue long sleeved shirt, conservative tie, and polished, dark shoes. For women, fashionably conservative is appropriate. For example, dress slacks or a longer skirt with a light colored blouse and a blazer. Women should avoid plunging necklines. The crucial element here is that every item of apparel be clean and pressed.

- Buy or borrow some type of leather-appearing portfolio that can hold your resume on one side and a pad of paper on the other.

- Bring a black pen that writes well and doesn't have the end chewed off.

- If you have piercings, remove the hardware, unless you're interviewing in that industry.

- Adhere to the personal hygiene guidelines mentioned in Chapter 5.

A cardinal rule is never to go into an interview without researching the company first. The people interviewing you will be able to detect if you haven't a clue about what the company does. With the Internet at your disposal, there isn't any excuse for not knowing about the company. What you hear during your interview will make more sense to you if you've investigated them before you show up at their door. And if doesn't make any sense, you can ask how the position you're interviewing for fits into the company's goals. Maybe you're being hired into a new division that hasn't been announced on their website, or perhaps they have plans to spin off or startup a new company.

- You'll be given directions and a time to show up at some location. *Never, ever, be late!* And do not show up an hour early. Ten to fifteen minutes is fine.

- If necessary, do a drive-by earlier in the week or verify the location via one of the internet mapping applications, and always allow for traffic disasters. Arriving at the company ten minutes before your appointed time is fine. They can make you wait but that's their prerogative as the employer, not yours, as the candidate. If you arrive earlier than necessary you can drive around or park in the back of the parking lot to wait it out.

- When you enter the lobby of the office building, you may be greeted by a security guard or a receptionist. Politely, and with a friendly look on your face, tell this person your name and who your appointment is with. He will tell you to have a seat. Don't slouch, and to calm your nerves, pick from the selection of outdated magazines left for you to peruse. Maybe they'll give you an application or visitor's badge to fill out. The guard may engage you with chit-chat. Don't act conceited; speak with him or her and be friendly and share comments on the weather. Don't be too preoccupied with your pending importance with this company. Why, you ask? That person may be good friends with your boss-to-be. Maybe he lives next door to him, or their kids play together, or they may go to the same place of worship. Realize that this person might see your interviewer-boss several times a day. So if you act self-important and arrogant, hope that this lowly person who isn't deserving of your time doesn't tell anyone about ". . . the stand-offish kid who showed up at 9:00."

- Someone will eventually show up to fetch you and extend their hand in greeting. When you greet someone, try to look them in the eye. Not with a "don't mess with me" stare, but conveying a friendly-serious-sincere feeling. When meeting women this is especially true. It is part of men's natural instinct to look elsewhere, but in the corporate world, aim for the eyes.

- Try and remember name of the person you just met. Repeat his/her name back to them in your return greeting to them: "Nice to meet you _____." If they mumbled or if it's a real tongue twister, you can ask them to repeat it, have them write it down, or you might have to let it go with just a "Nice to meet you." Later on, when you're being handed off to someone else, you can ask for his/her business card or ask them how his/her name is spelled; have your pen ready to write it down (or have them do it.) You can even ask the second person you meet the name of the person you initially spoke to.

- With handshakes, don't give the other person your hand and expect them to do all the work, commonly referred to as the "dead fish." If you are unsure about the health of your fish, practice your handshake with a man and woman whose opinion you value. Both genders should give a firm handshake with their full hand.

- On the other end of the spectrum, fracturing someone's phalanges won't get you a job offer unless you're trying to land a Mixed Martial Arts role. The technique is firm: not crushing, not wet noodle.

- If your hands sweat, keep them open and facing up on your lap while you're speaking. Don't clutch a tissue in your hands.

- Nail biting or picking at your cuticles during the interview doesn't make a positive impression because it conveys anxiety and nervousness.

In the real world, people don't usually rely on their titles. The only person at work that I ever addressed as "Dr." was a self-important, pompous person. Usually, it's first names. Except in the military, of course, and in the medical field. If, however, someone says that they're going to take you down to hall "…to meet Mr. Cheesebreath", then you know to address him by Mr. If he wants you to be more familiar, he'll tell you his first name and ask that you address him as such. Sir or ma'am also works in an ambiguous situation.

You'll probably start the interview in someone's office, perhaps an HR representative, or someone with whom you will be working. People might stick their heads in or he/she may be paged to take an urgent phone call or handle a crisis. Glance away and wait. Some interviews are not rigidly structured, but throughout it, pay attention to what you see and hear and try to get an accurate picture of the organization. I remember an informal interview I had where the manager's wife called him to report on his son's poor behavior. They went back and forth and finally, after the second call on this issue he said "Just give him a good slap, okay?"

If they mention something that you recognize, say so, and act "alive." I've spoken to some candidates who I thought froze into a pillar of salt. I'd be explaining this and that and they would be just staring at me—not nodding their heads in understanding or showing any body movement. I wanted to hold a mirror under their noses to see if they were breathing. You don't want to be a jittering bundle of flesh, either.

If you see a computer aided design center, you can ask what software they use. If you pass the marketing department, ask if they regularly have a booth at trade shows. If they say yes, you can ask which ones. They might mention one at McCormick Center in Chicago and then you can ask how successful the show was for them. If Chicago is your home town or you visited it, you might ask if they had a chance to patronize a particular restaurant or see the Chagall mosaic. My point is for you to show:

- That you are personable and knowledgeable
- That you can communicate
- That you can relate to others beyond the scope of your job. This means that you have a personality and are not just an automaton who works without regard to the people around him

---

Asking questions shows you're actively listening and thinking about what you're being told. Repeatedly saying "Uh-huh" can leave people with the feeling that you're hearing but not necessarily understanding what they're saying. Some interactivity or dialogue is beneficial; it helps you connect with the people you're speaking with.

Try not to let the whole affair be a big blur. Yes, you're on the spot, meeting new people in an unfamiliar location, and nearly suffocating with a shirt buttoned to the top and a tie or a conservative dress that made your roommate inquire if you were joining a religious order. But you have to get some idea if this is where you want to work. You'll be spending at least forty hours there every week. Can you see yourself getting up in the morning and driving there?

- Remember: *you're also interviewing them.*
- Ask *"Why is this position available?"* It's nice to know if someone resigned, was promoted, or if this is a newly created position.
- Ask *"What qualities or skills are you looking for in the ideal candidate?"*
- Ask *"What is a typical day like?"*
- Ask *"What is the performance evaluation process?"* You want to know when you'll have your first evaluation or performance review and how often they occur.
- Ask *"How does the group I'm interviewing for interact with other groups in the company?"* This will give you a bigger picture view of the organization.
- Ask about the learning curve for the job. How fast do they expect you to come up to speed? Will you be sent someplace for training?
- If you feel that you especially fit what they mention, tell them, but be sure you are able to justify your answer.

  For example, *"I feel I would be an excellent tax accountant for many reasons: For two years I assisted students at my college preparing their tax returns. I was considered quite knowledgeable among my peers in changes to the tax laws. Of course, I'm extremely detail-oriented and have the stamina to put in the extra hours during the tax season. From what I've seen today, your company is exactly what I'm looking for; I hope you feel the same about me."*
- You can make clear your enthusiasm and desire for the job. Granted it puts them on the spot a little, but your interest comes across loud and clear. All you have to say is *"I am very interested in this position and hope that you will consider making me an offer."* Most likely they'll mention that they have to evaluate all the candidates but they will appreciate your interest and know where you stand.

- Even though you'll likely be interviewing for a paid position, it's not the candidate's place to *initiate* a discussion of salary. You should, however, have some idea of what is a fair wage for the position you're interviewing for, and take into consideration the cost of living where the job is located. An extremely modest shack on the west coast will cost much, much more than palatial surroundings on the east side of the U.S. Even on the east coast, the cost of living varies greatly; an apartment in New York City or Boston will be more than one in upstate New York. Similarly, don't bring up benefits, vacation, holidays, and other perks until you receive an offer from them. Stay focused on the job.

During the actual interview, when they're showing you around or speaking to you about the position:

- Pay attention
- Tell the truth
- Project your competence in your field, a willingness to learn, work hard, get along with your coworkers and be an above average performer.
- Find out what is expected of the person who accepts the position. All employers would like any candidate to be able to step into the job on their first day and hit the ground running, but if you at least have initiative and dedication, and are not afraid to ask a question you have more than enough to get you going.

Any interview you have is successful if you come out of it understanding if the position is right for you. Completing an interview and realizing that a particular job or company is not one you would want to work at or for is beneficial for both you and the company. If a job isn't a perfect fit with what you are looking for, it's not unheard-of to settle for the opportunity closest to your goal. Just don't waste your time or that of a potential employer.

Many people go about their jobs and realize that work is filled with ups and downs, slow periods and hectic ones, creative, productive times and doldrums. The important thing is not to *dread* going to work. Some days you might not look forward to it because there is an unpleasant task you have to do or a difficult person to meet with. But when dread becomes a way of life, if you start the day with an expletive when your alarm clock goes off, start to pay attention and find out what's wrong. If you're miserable at your job, it can be difficult to make up for it with your life outside of work. Why? Because you just can't turn it off at five o'clock.

Scientists use the term *half-life* which is the time required for an amount of decaying (radioactive) material to decrease by half. Values for half-lives can vary from millionths of a second to over 24,000 years for the element plutonium. A job you don't like has a half-life of many hours, so that it could take several hours for you to decompress or put aside your discontent. And during those several hours, you could be doing things much more enjoyable than sulking or feeling badly and wishing for a change. In addition, it's difficult to perform well at a job you can't stand. The whole situation becomes a vicious downward spiral.

Is there room for your ambition?

Healthy organizations want their people to have ambition. Towards the end of the interview, when things seem to be winding down, or in a second interview, you can broach the question of your ambition in many different ways.

The best approach is to ask the question directly: *"Looking down the road, what opportunities for promotion or paths for advancement are there for someone with my education?"*

Another way is to say *"I feel that it's valuable during someone's career to gain experience in different parts of a company. Where else in the corporation are (marketing assistants, software developers, accountants, or 'people with my qualifications') employed?"* You have to ask what additional education may be required. Perhaps an MBA is looked upon favorably. At some point you can inquire if the company will reimburse you for education. You may want to know if there is a point in your career where you can head towards management of a group, or advance as an individual contributor. The key points you want to understand are what directions an ambitious person, pending the other necessary qualifications—like excellent performance reviews, solid expertise, and good leadership skills—can achieve.

Remember: No matter how desperate you are for a job, you have to interview the company. The ball isn't totally in their court: They may extend an offer to you, and, if you feel that you would not enjoy the position or dislike some aspect of the company, you can, and should, refuse it. Ask yourself—and be honest in your answer— if you can see yourself there for twenty years or only five. Sometimes a job is a stepping stone.

Giving thanks

As soon as possible after an interview you should write a thank-you note to the person who would be your direct boss and any other main players you met. While some people feel that if you are not interested in the position, there is no need to write a thank-you note, my stance is that it is a simple courtesy and it is always viewed as positive by the recipient. You should:

- Thank the interviewer for his/her time and for considering you for the position—and name the position specifically. Or you can mention that you enjoyed meeting him or her and discussing the opportunities with the company. Mention your interest in the position.

- Tell him/her again why you feel that you have the skills to do the job. It's all about selling yourself. For example, if you had a summer job working for their direct competitor reiterate that and mention how you already have experience with their business and terminology.
- Finally, state that you look forward to hearing from him/her and close the letter in the appropriate fashion.
- Keep the note brief and to the point; you just don't want them to forget you. Send a note out for every job you interview for, even if the job isn't at the top of your list. Perhaps you interviewed for a position you weren't especially interested in but another division with a different job that is more appealing to you recently opened up. You don't know what can happen. Play to win so that you can dictate your path.

I favor email over the postal service because it's as close to immediate as possible. Whatever method you choose, *proof this note very carefully* because that will be their last impression of you.

Later in the day, you should also replay the entire interview in your mind and write down—as best as you are able—who you met, what they told you, what they asked you, *your reply to what they asked you,* where they took you, and how you felt about each part of the meeting. This provides you with documentation that will prepare you for the next interview you will have. Did you give a response to a question that seemed to puzzle the interviewer? For example, you might have felt on the spot if, for instance, someone asked you how deeply your economics course covered Keynesian theories, what textbook you used in organic chemistry, or why you feel qualified to work for their company. Unfortunately you cannot prepare for every question but you can try to *remain calm* and *answer the question as best you can.*

If the main thing you remember from economics is the joy of

earning a passing grade, you can say that you recall covering that topic in class, but you're not prepared to discuss it in any detail. That will probably suffice, unless you majored in economics. Recalling the author of a textbook you used may seem unrealistic, but if the person who asked teaches part-time he/she may have a special interest. You can say that you cannot recall the author but that you found the book contained excellent explanations/was incomprehensible/didn't have any answers in the back of the book for you to check your attempts at the problems.

Negotiating an offer

When companies want to extend you an offer, they will say something like "Oscar, we would like to offer you an entry-level position as a widget wizard at Fabulous Flanges, reporting to Mr. Cheesebreath. We are offering you a salary of one million dollars paid semi-monthly. Attached to this note is a document detailing our benefits package. Please let us know as soon as possible if you accept this offer."

Your response to this should be something to this effect: "I am pleased to hear from you with this offer. It certainly sounds like a wonderful opportunity. I will need time to review the offer and get back to you with any questions.

Once you have all the information about the offer, think carefully about the factors important to you. Here are what many consider to be the top three:

- Salary
- Vacation
- Benefits

From your research you should know how much entry-level employees in your field are earning. OK, great—ask for more. Scared they may shy away from you? Any company that rescinds an offer because you asked for a modest increase in your starting salary wouldn't be a company that you would want to work for, would it? Research the top end of the salary curve for your field and ask for as much of that amount as you are comfortable with. Keep in mind the location of the company—living costs can vary from coast to coast. One way of phrasing this request is "Would you be able increase the compensation offered to me by ten percent per year?" They may counter it with a lower offer, or mention that new employees generally receive a salary increase after completing a sales training course or attaining some other milestone. Don't be shy—after all, we all know what will happen if you don't ask, right? (The answer is *nothing*.) You may or may not get what you ask for, but you *won't* get what you *don't* ask for. No one (except for your mom) can read your mind. Be upfront and matter-of-fact. Maybe they'll have to get back to you and who knows what they will say— but at least you asked.

An employer may counter your request for higher salary by mentioning the value of their benefits package. You might hear the phrase "total compensation or salary" meaning that the value of the benefits package can be added to your salary. And this is very true: medical insurance is very expensive, and if you marry and have dependents, the cost to the company (and you, of course) increases. One thing to remember: when you are buying groceries, the check-out clerk doesn't care what your benefits are. You cannot use them as tender for your debts. So if you ask for an increase in your starting salary and you receive a lecture on how wonderful the benefits are, you can say that while you realize that and are grateful for them, you would like them to address the base salary.

Vacation will take on a whole new meaning once you are gainfully employed. Gone are the days when you can catch a nap after classes or have a long lunch because your next class isn't until two o'clock. The holiday when there was no classes will now be just another workday. If you don't have the vacation time, you may even have to work Christmas Eve and the day after Christmas. It can be a particularly brutal awakening; it was for me.

It isn't *incorrect* to ask for and receive an extra week's vacation. It's not uncommon for a new employee to get two weeks' vacation that is increased to three, four, five and six weeks after five, ten, fifteen and twenty years of service. Get approval for additional vacation in writing. You may also inquire if it is possible to buy a week's vacation. Companies will deduct the cost of that extra week from your paycheck, sometimes over the course of a year, which takes some of the monetary sting out. Of course, vacation isn't discussed until *after* you receive an offer.

Uncle Frank's Theory of Time Acceleration: A tongue-in-cheek summary

Once you are employed, you will become aware of this phenomenon. I haven't heard anyone else speak about it, so I claim it as my concept. Though not as complicated as Albert Einstein's Special and General Theories of Relativity, it is all too real and experienced by everyone in the world of work. It's quite simple to comprehend: the passage of time increases dramatically as we distance ourselves from the workplace. After you are employed, a two day weekend, for instance, will appear on Friday afternoon to be two glorious fun-filled days of freedom. Yet as soon as you awaken Saturday morning, time will appear to accelerate so much so that unexpectedly, it will be the tail end of Sunday evening with Monday morning coming up fast. The rate of time acceleration will increase with your distance from the workplace and is inversely proportional to the enjoyment you experience: a week-long cruise to a far-away exotic island with the love of your life will seem to be over a day or two after it begins, but three days spent with boring relatives will appear to last for two weeks. An alcohol-infused weekend with your buddies from school? Why go, as it will appear to be over in a matter of hours. Two hours selecting furniture, carpeting, and drapery with your companion? Equivalent to about a day and a half at the minimum.

Chapter 5
Contract Employment

A common concern among newly minted graduates is where to get the experience that all the employers seem to want. One way to get experience is to apply to *contract* or *temporary employment* agencies. As a contract employee

- You are employed by one company to work at another company
- It's a method for companies to get temporary help; they get a warm body to do the work and when it's done, so is the person who did the work.

- The worker can also be shown the door if the project ends prematurely or for any reason they can think of, including conflict between the contract employee and the people he works with.

- While the contract agency may pay some meager benefits, the company where the work is being done does not.

- The contract agency is paid by the company for the work you do. The agency takes their cut and gives you the rest.

Some people compare this to the world's oldest profession, but *for you* it's a way to get experience. In addition,

- With a contract position, you will likely interview directly with the person for whom you'll be working, so you bypass HR and, for better or worse, any hiring demographics they are supposed to adhere to.

- Your benefits, holiday pay and other perks will be minimal.

- Your hourly wage will likely be lower than what a "direct" employee at the company would earn.

- You get some work experience and possibly some excellent references. A favorable reference is priceless because you've got an advocate for your competence and ability to get along with people.

The responsibilities assigned to contracts are more of along the lines of "We need this done, so please just do it" as opposed to the grooming of a new employee. Generally, when you're newly hired you may not receive any true deliverables (tasks to complete in a timely manner) for some time. You may be given things to read or review before you do anything that can be called work. As a contract employee you can expect that they'll point out the location of the restrooms and after a brief overview, put you to work on a task. It varies from place to place, of course.

- Remember that you can make any assignment, no matter how monotonous, a valuable reflection of your work ethic and competence.

- As a contract employee, you won't appear on the company payrolls, therefore you might be treated differently than regular employees; in fact, you might feel like a second-class citizen at times. Choose to view contracting as a means to get experience and then transition to a "regular" or "direct" job either within the same company or somewhere else.

- Use it to help you decide if you like a particular field of endeavor. Like any job, you can resign, but keep in mind that the contracting agency does not want people who will flit from job to job. They are in it for the same reason we all are: to make money. So you can't use them as a vehicle for soul searching. If you do want to try a variety of jobs, stress that you are seeking short-term temporary employment.

Act professional, keep your opinions about the company to yourself, do the best job you can, and try your absolute best to get along with everyone. It's not what many consider an ideal situation. It may not seem fair that you have to prostitute yourself in order to get experience so that *eventually* you can earn a decent living, but the world is not a fair place. For the most part, you *make your own* fortune. . . and misfortune.

Some companies tend to string along contract workers because they're cheap labor and usually don't appear in the head count on personnel rosters. Because a contract agency is sometimes paid with a purchase order—the same form used for new equipment—contract employees are invisible in the organizational structure, and are thought of as a tool for getting the work done. Contract workers may show up under expenses in the budget. This isn't a cozy picture, but remember, once you get inside a company, even as a contract worker, you can explore. For example, if part of your responsibility is to deliver prototype flanges to the testing lab, you have a great view of what that particular department is all about. Should you see someone from the testing department in the cafeteria, and with the nodding acquaintance you may develop with him/her, you can ask to join him/her at their lunch table and begin relating to him/her on a friend-from-work level.

You don't want your agency or the company you're contracting at to give you the spiel ". . . be grateful you have a job. . . the economy is so tight in your field" and so on. I'm sure you are grateful to have a job, and you'll put aside the shortcomings of contracting and do the best you can — but when you can make a break for a better, direct position within a company or anywhere else for that matter, go for it. As hard-nosed as it may sound, you have to think of yourself first.

Generally, people are accommodating towards a young, earnest, ambitious contract worker's quest for a "real" job in the company, so you shouldn't hesitate to ask people you meet at your job for help in finding long-term opportunities. You don't want to start sniffing around right from the get-go or come on too strong, lest your eagerness is perceived by your co-workers as threatening. Get into the job, learn the lay of the land and after a couple months of doing your absolute best, begin to branch out. It's almost like a covert military mission but without the camouflage and explosions.

When your contract ends, you don't want to be set adrift, unless you are grateful to be gone which is sometimes the case.

If you disliked the job, try to leave on favorable terms. In any event, there is a silver lining: You now know

- What to look for in a boss.
- What to look for in a job.
- What to avoid in future opportunities that made your most recent one unsatisfactory.

Another avenue to consider is a traditional employment agency that deals with permanent (which is a term you don't hear much with the word employment) positions or better said, not short-term contractual positions. Like any agency, they play both sides of the field and try to match a company with an employee, but the amount of money at stake for the headhunter is much greater. They are usually compensated with a negotiated percentage of the starting salary of the candidate, who must stay at the company for a designated period of time in order for the agency to be paid by *the company the candidate is placed*. NEVER deal with any agency that wants money from you, no matter what they promise.

Other resourceful measures

I would be remiss if I didn't tell you that for some individuals, the path to a first career can be a jagged one, fraught with cliffs leading to deep abysses, along with some frustration, and, unfortunately, disappointment. Job searches have ups and downs.

As ridiculous or difficult as it sounds, a major goal is to try to remain optimistic: job hunting is a numbers game. It's akin to standing on the street corner and asking passersby if they would give you a dollar. Ask enough people and someone will oblige, though I've never tried this myself. The same goes for job hunting. If you look long enough, you will find a job, but there may be contingencies. You have to be ready to compromise, sometimes on many fronts. Your dream job in an attractive locale with a kingpin in an industry may have to be postponed until later in your career. Perhaps you *will* land in a different type of city than you envisioned, but you may meet the love of your life there, or there will be more opportunities for growth, or any one of many positive results.

Sometimes people close to you, when hearing that you were offered a position that you are not thrilled with, may say for you to "make the best of it" This is akin to saying to someone that an impending thirty-year prison sentence will give them time to catch up on their reading. What they mean is that you should look for the positive and strive to do your best—it won't be the first time in your life that you will have to compromise.

Remember during your job search to keep networking. Be creatively bold. For example, suppose you want to get your resume in front of someone at a modest-sized company, but you are only able to get as far as the receptionist at the front door. Handing her your resume with an inexpensive hand-held flower arrangement (~ $10) is certainly worth a try. Or a small box of candy. Maybe your attempts to contact someone are intercepted by his administrative assistant. You can try leveling with him/her. "I've been trying to connect with Mr. Cheesebreath for an exploratory interview, but it's proving to be difficult. I'm a new graduate, and honestly, your company is my number one target employer. If I sent you my resume would you put it on Mr. Cheesebreath's desk?" Or perhaps you get an "I'm on vacation" message from someone. If their message leaves someone's name to contact, go ahead and connect with them and ask them when the person you're interested in is returning, or even if they know anything about an open job posting. Got it?—BE BOLD!! There are no rules!

Sooner or later, you will land someplace. If there were people who gave you outstanding references, made you aware of opportunities, or steered you in the right direction, be sure to thank him/her for being in your corner. Send a card or at the very least an email, and once in a while, send a note to say hello and share what you are doing, Don't forget him/her.

Uncle Frank's story—if you're curious

After I graduated from college in the mid 1970s (yes, I'm likely older than your father) I started graduate school at a university in Massachusetts. I stayed there only a year; the simple explanation is that I wasn't ready for the demands of graduate school. So I returned to my hometown and my parents' house with my ego, confidence and dreams bruised, and started to look for a job. It was a difficult time economically, and finding a job was challenging. I felt the need to be near my support system (family) which limited my options. After six months I was offered a job in quality control at a local pharmaceutical company. The department I worked in was responsible for analyzing the finished products headed to the marketplace to ensure the active ingredient was present in the advertised amount. My salary was low. In fact, when I received the phone call with the job offer, I accepted on the spot. My father overheard the conversation and after I hung up, he mentioned that I should have considered asking them to let me think about it for a day or two and possibly ask for more money. This shocked me, as my family was anxious for me to get to work and be productive, so I thought that if an offer came my way, I should accept it immediately. This turned out to be a big, big mistake.

I showed up for work at eight and before nine o'clock I was on the bench starting to learn the ins and outs of analyzing drugs. I didn't even know where the restroom was. It was a big lab with three other men and about nine or ten women. The work wasn't that exciting—it was boring as hell to me and I soon realized that I had made a mistake accepting the position. The other half of the story is that I really didn't have my act together back then. I was immature, had some unresolved issues, and didn't realize that it was *just a job*. It didn't have to rule me, or define me. I just had to do it, collect the money, and search for something better if I didn't like it. It wasn't a bad job, as there weren't any terrible hazards, and people weren't collapsing from exhaustion. There were adequate surroundings with friendly people. Lousy pay, but then I was fresh out of school.

I remember best the loathing I had for this job, the absolute *dread* that filled my soul when morning came and the unbounded joy when the clock finally made its way to five. This is what I referred to earlier as a long half-life. The problem was that I hated it so much that shortly after the day was over or the weekend had begun, I would start to dread going back to work. I hated it in *advance*. What a sad state of mental anguish! I quit after four months (and five days), precisely what many people advised me *not* to do. I credit the hatred I had for that job for my master's degree. I needed to escape from that job, and what better place than the warm bosom of academia.

A couple years later, with my newly minted master's degree, I set out to re-enter the workforce, only to find that the economic climate in town had not recovered that much. Companies that advised me a few years earlier that I would be more attractive with an advanced degree now deemed me as overqualified.

My big break was being hired for a seven-week contract position while an employee was out for surgery. I networked with people I met at the company and found a second contract position to follow the first but written for just six months. That contract position ended and was followed by a third position (in another group down the hall from the second position) written for a year!

The company, however, was slowly descending into a period of massive downsizing and restructuring. I was assured by all my managers that I was being "released" (a nice word for prematurely ending my contract) purely due to economic reasons. Their references were valuable for attaining a fourth contract about a year later in an entirely different part of the same company.

After six months of unemployment (I was still reluctant to relocate), I landed a position within a local governmental agency that was responsible for the monitoring and control of water pollution. My job was in the lab, and paid substantially less than my previous job. And I *hated it*. It was an easy job, but as a civil service position, it seemed that there was no room to grow or move around unless someone died. It was secure. The people were nice. Local government is kind of persnickety when it comes to purchasing common supplies for the lab: everything had to go out for three bids. This drove me crazy, because it is so bureaucratic. One of my bosses was, to be polite, an *interesting* fellow, and I'll mention him later. It seemed that there wasn't any energy at this job—no senior scientists to interact with, no encouragement of innovation, and no incentive to excel. For example, in industry, if you consistently give much more in your job than what is expected, you might eventually be promoted or be given an award or recognized in some fashion. There wasn't any of that here. Leave on time, stay for an extra two hours—no big deal, unless you claimed overtime. Then there were approvals, forms to be signed, etc. After I was there about a year, I received a call from a contract recruiter about a position where I had previously worked. It was a *six-month* contract, but I jumped at the chance to interview and was offered the job. So after exactly fifty-three weeks, I left this secure position in local government for a fourth contract position in a new exciting area of the company where I had the previous three contracts. The money was twice what I was currently earning, but however, it wasn't as secure as I would have liked. But I was determined to get a different job. I had essentially no responsibilities except for a small car loan and monthly apartment rent. I calculated that with my salary from the contract job and that of a part-time job I had as a teaching assistant for an evening chemistry lab, I could save enough money to pay my expenses for six months if the contract job was not renewed for another six month period. I figured that if I could not make it after a year, perhaps Casa Mom and Dad would still have my room available.

I started the fourth contract at an interesting time. Most of the entire group had just received accolades for several technical successes. They received monetary awards and their photographs were taken and hung in the hallway for everyone to admire. People were smiling and slapping each other on the back. It was quite impressive and I congratulated them on their achievements. While you may be tempted to call this "sucking up", people like to be recognized for good things that have happened to them. You don't have to make a big deal of it, just a sincere *"Congratulations on your award, Simon."* There's no need to go on and on with your praise. That can dilute your kind thoughts to become indistinguishable from insincerity, which, once detected, is a tough label to shake off.

The project I was on was in advanced development, which meant that when management had confidence in it being a successful product, it would become an official product program. Unfortunately, there were problems with the technology and it appeared that the project would not advance to become a product. The problems were quite apparent because people were leaving the project like rats on a sinking ship and finding other jobs, both within and outside of the company. Whenever someone that I interacted with departed for greener pastures, I approached them and asked if I could use them as a reference in my search for a permanent position, and if so, would their reference would be favorable. If you have the sense to ask the right people, you always get a yes, which was also the case with me. I also gave them a few copies of my resume and told them that if they knew of any positions that were suitable for someone with my skills to please let me know or give their new manager a copy of my resume (this was when email and the Internet were still a dream.)

After several months of this style of networking, I received a call from a particularly brilliant scientist who had left the project a few months earlier. He described to me two positions and asked me which one I was interested in. Soon after, I interviewed and was offered a position. My career hasn't been a fairy tale: there have been plenty of challenging situations but a lot of successes too.

Chapter 6
Your Job, Reality, and the Compromise

"Do what you like, like what you do."
– Motto of the Life is Good ® clothing company

We see the naivety of the boy in the cartoon, thinking that his job will always be enjoyable.

When it comes to earning a living, the definition of fun changes. Work is *not always fun* but it shouldn't be drudgery. I think the essentials of a tolerable job are that you:

- Use your skills and knowledge
- Have challenges to help you reach out of your comfort zone
- Are adequately compensated
- Have tolerable and pleasant coworkers
- Have an ethical and competent supervisor
- Have a warm, dry, safe and secure place to work

I'll be talking in this section about how to deal with your job it if it isn't the passion you've dreamt of. Let's begin with an important concept you have to realize about the world of work: **it's not going to be fair.** The higher you ascend in the company ranks, the fairer it will be with respect to yourself, of course. The minions, and by that word I'm referring to everyone who isn't on a bonus plan, will receive less perks than the managers.

---

*"Expecting the world to treat you fairly because you are
a good person is a little like expecting the bull not to attack you
because you are a vegetarian." — Dennis Wholey*

For example, your company may have, through no fault of yours, some periods of poorer-than-expected financial performance. The president, CEO, CFO, or other big wheel may send out a note announcing that due to the poor financials there will be no raises in pay, or the company will no longer contribute matching funds to your 401-k, or there may be downsizings or layoffs, spending will be curtailed, product launches canceled or something else that will cost you money. Those in the upper echelon will not be affected that much. They will still be enjoying perks of their job, but at a reduced level. Their quarterly bonuses may be 10% instead of 20%, they may need approval before they use a company chauffeur or private plane, or heaven forbid, their stock options may be cut. Oh, the horror. I try not to think of this, as it makes my blood boil. It is an inequality that exists because there is no other choice than to find another job at a different company. Or start your own company.

In some companies, the boss's offspring may rapidly ascend the ranks, or fresh from school, become sales managers over people who have many years in the trenches. The boss's offspring may get summer jobs or internships in comfortable environments and return to school with accolades for their memorable performance even though they may have been a lazy pain in the ass. No one wants to risk career suicide by letting the boss know that their offspring needs to learn what a work ethic is. Not that it would make any difference because they are still anointed.

And we are almost powerless to do anything about it. Sure, you can vote with your feet and leave the company, but if you enjoy what you are doing, why make things difficult for yourself? The fact is that this goes on everywhere. Life in general may not seem to be fair. Fairness and the randomness of misfortune are never hand-in-hand. There is, however one person that you can count on to be fair, and that is YOU. Be a *solid* person. Being solid is being genuine, not someone who tells partial truths or who is always looking for the easy way out. They do the right thing, even if they are the only one who will know of it. There is more about solid people in the next chapter.

Mixed feelings

It took me a while to get used to the idea of work. There aren't any semester or summer breaks, during the holidays you get only one or two days off, and not showing up because you just don't feel like it isn't acceptable. It's an awakening experience to have to put on adult attire and report for duty.

I venture to say that close to 100% of people, when asked if there was anything else they would be doing as work would not hesitate to answer affirmatively. Hopefully this excludes medical personnel, air traffic controllers, police, and firefighters. This isn't to say that everyone hates their job, but it's fair to say that from time to time, most people would admit to not preferring *some aspect* of it. I think that's why it's called *work*. If you truly *despise* many of aspects your job, it's time to do some serious thinking about your state of mind, in addition to the job. Although you may think a particular job is worthless, it's important to someone and needs to be done well. When the trash collectors go on strike, everyone is grateful when they return to work.

Unfortunately, not everyone gets the opportunity to work in the area they're passionate about. I might be wrong, but I've always thought that musicians and artists are passionate about their degrees because they have to give so much of themselves, and their direction after school is more defined (I think) than someone with a degree in Business Administration or Physics, who has so many potential avenues to pursue. I mean if you major in music, then you'll probably make music or be involved with music in some fashion. The downside is that you cannot, in many cases, count on a regular paycheck pursuing that passion.

If you are unsure about where you want to begin your working life, I believe that the very best book to guide you towards discovering the sweet spot of your skills and passions is *What Color is Your Parachute* by Richard N. Bolles. Bolles' book, like a fine wine, has gotten better and better over time. The important thing to remember is that only *you* know what you want to do. A book can only guide you, with all the input coming from you, to bring the answers to your conscious mind. It's not like doing your taxes where you can be reasonably assured that if you have all the necessary information and follow the directions, by the end of the second page you'll know where you stand. Beyond the exercises in this book there is a considerable amount of soul-searching that requires you be aware of your goals and to continually hone your thoughts to a sharper image of where that intersection of career-passion-make-a-living is in your life.

Managing your job versus your hobby

Can you be passionate about your work *and* your hobby? Absolutely. I've worked with many individuals who, on their own time, have made beautiful furniture, taken breathtaking photographs, done miraculous restorations on automobiles, and even built entire houses from the ground up and have successful, productive careers. The key is knowing how to separate your job from your hobby or *avocation* and set your priorities. If you've stayed up late to put the finishing touches on the walnut armoire but are wiped out the next day at your big meeting at Fabulous Flanges, you need to reexamine your priorities. Generally, the job finances the hobby, so the former takes precedence. Your employer expects you to have outside interests but being more interested in your hobby than your job sends the wrong message.

For most of us, we begin to understand early in our working lives that it's a matter of compromise: you have to like what you do, but you have to earn a living. So it wouldn't be the *worst* situation if initially you could *tolerate* what you're doing. I'm not telling you to "get tough with yourself and suck it up" at something you're going to be miserable at. Remember what I said about the half-life of a job you hate. Whatever the situation, consider it an opportunity to discover what you *don't* want to do for a living. It will help if you are open-minded enough to consider any and all options.

For example, suppose you have a newly minted degree in psychology and are resistant to attending graduate school. But you like helping people through difficult times and realize that people who have just experienced the loss of a loved one need someone to guide them. Somehow you begin to think of the profession of funeral director. Your initial aversion could be overcome with the realization of how recession-resistant that occupation is and the degree of comfort and care you can provide to the decedents' family at such an emotionally difficult time. In New York State, this career goal requires at least two years of study in order to be licensed. Granted, an occupation dependent on people dying may not seem appealing to some people you meet, but that is their problem, not yours.

Chapter 7
Courtesy and Consideration

"Our character is what we do when we think no one is looking."
– H. Jackson Browne, Jr.

"Do good and forget; do bad and remember."
– Rose Cosentino Pagano, my maternal grandmother

A significant portion of your success at work will hinge on how you act and the relationship you have with your colleagues. Extreme competence, short of brilliance, doesn't guarantee you rocketing ascension in the company. You will encounter people who aren't necessarily the sharpest knives in the drawer who are managers, and unbelievably gifted people who have modest positions. And you'll see the exact opposite. The point is that your interactions and ability to work with other people can influence your progress in the workplace.

In this chapter you will see that I'm not shy about mentioning issues that others may not mention. And as situations vary, you may have to modify your response.

Creating a solid foundation

Of all the advice I offer in these pages, the most important one—the keystone to advancement—the crucial principle—*that I implore you to remember for your entire working life*—is this: Strive for perfect attendance unless you are truly ill or injured or have previously scheduled vacation.

Yes, you probably have sick days and I'll talk about them later, but remember this: you were hired to help the company make money by performing certain tasks they feel essential to their business. Companies are schedule-driven: product has to ship, inventory has to be maintained, testing has to be completed, accounts have to reconciled, right? You contribute to one or more of these items and if you're not there, the schedule slips which can cost the company considerably if, for example, a customer cancels their business relationship with the company you work for to go with the competition. When you schedule vacation time, your manager takes your absence into account and adjusts the productivity accordingly, or may be forced to do your job— and his—himself. You may *think* you are not that important and your presence doesn't affect the company significantly—and you are *incorrect* in thinking that.

Let me explain it this way: recall the song you might have sung as a child that goes like this: "...the leg bone is connected to the knee bone, the knee bone is connected to the shin bone, the shin bone is connected to the foot bone...." The world of work isn't substantially different. Research drives engineering, engineering drives production, production drives sales, sales drive profitability, which drives accounting, and so on. The success of a company is synergistic: it depends on many interrelated factors, one of them which is *your job*.

One final imploration: NEVER, EVER be absent from work without notifying your supervisor by phone and email you will not be there. Just not showing up, can be grounds for immediate dismissal.

The basics

Every day, you need to pay attention to your overall cleanliness and hygiene. I realize that during the pressures of school you may have taken certain shortcuts.

- Shower with soap and use underarm deodorant every day.
- Regularly brush and floss your teeth and use a mouthwash.
- Have decayed teeth repaired. Advancements in painless and affordable dentistry have made this more palatable (pun intended).
- Use cotton-tipped swabs daily to clean your ear canal.
- Gentlemen, even if your daily beard growth isn't substantial, shave every day. Don't come to work looking like you spent the night in jail.
- Go easy on the perfume, cologne or aftershave. If you slather it on, olfactory fatigue makes you smell the fragrance less and less, while those around you are asphyxiated.
- Thoroughly wash your hands with soap and water after you use the restroom, no matter how meticulous and careful you are. This applies everywhere, not just where others may see you skip out. Of course, this is standard hygienic practice and besides, people notice and remember who doesn't and when the topic comes up, your name will be mentioned. Those in the know will probably shun any food you bring in to share, and inform others.

Some people's habits may not align with contemporary hygiene. This is a sad truth about life. I witnessed one fellow proceed to gargle and spit into the coffee area sink. The only way to handle this (I didn't want to confront him) was to put a sign over the sink which said in large red capital letters "DO NOT SPIT IN THE SINK. USE THE RESTROOM." It took care of it.

- Keep your fingers away from your nostrils.

- Blowing your nose should be done away from the lunch or dinner table. Don't be the person who, after finishing lunch at a table with his friends, pulls out a well-used handkerchief, blows loud enough to wake the dead, and then proceeds to examine it!

Regarding dressing for your job: it's probably best to avoid extremes and dress like everyone else. Sorry for the forthcoming mental image, but where I spent the majority of my work life I could probably have come in with a grass skirt and a couple of coconut shells on my chest, but as long as I did what I was supposed to, there would have been no problem. Other companies have dress codes, and if you want to work there, you've got to comply. If you're in one of the investment fields, you *have* to dress like you're the president of the company, because you're asking people to trust you with their money. First appearances count double or triple for you. Be aware that companies may not allow body art, in the form of tattoos or piercings *that are visible when you are dressed for work and if you are interacting face-to-face with customers*. Of course this depends on how much face time you will have with customers, what type of company you're working for, etc. So at a motorcycle shop, you'll probably be fine. At a tattoo/piercing shop, it will probably be a requirement. At a conservative institution, it might be acceptable but only if you are hidden in a remote room in the basement. With the ever-increasing popularity of body art companies are changing their policies.

Whatever you wear, cleanliness is the rule.

- The permanent press label on a shirt really means "minimal press." No matter how clean it is, don't pull a freshly laundered shirt from a pile and wear it without at least touching it up with an iron.
- Never wear any article of clothing that is stained. If you get caught between laundry days, consider disguising a marked piece

of apparel with a sweater. Chemists worked hard developing detergents that work wonders on the most stubborn stains.

During an interview with a company, observe everyone's attire and manner of dress, but on your first day, overdress a little— wear a tie and jacket, for example. Women should do something analogous to that. Your boss will tell you that you can lose the tie or whatever, but show up over-respectful to start.

With your colleagues, act like a responsible, considerate and courteous adult, even if the people around you don't.

- When your coffee cup leaves a ring, clean it up.

- If you spill coffee, especially if it's on the stairs, find a paper towel and mop it up before someone slips on it. You can ask someone for a couple of facial tissues to do the job.

- When you leave an office or conference room, tuck your chair back under the desk or table. Don't leave the room like a tornado hit it. Erase the board and sweep the bagel crumbs into the waste basket. When you leave a colleague's office after a discussion, put the visitors' chair you sat in back where you found it.

Hallway conversations, particularly near the coffee area or water cooler are commonplace in most organizations. In some workplaces, whiteboards with markers are placed to foster impromptu collaboration or discussion. In one building where I worked, there was one such area on each floor of the building and served as a hub of sorts. These spots can encourage friendly chatter or heated debates because the structure associated with the workplace is different: everyone is there to get coffee. It can foster innovative thinking and helpful discussions or just be a break from the daily routine.

- There are generally several pots containing or brewing what can be defined loosely as coffee. At times, it might seem to be the vilest tasting stuff and require a hefty dose of sweetener and creamer to choke down, but don't worry, it's an acquired taste. If you empty the pot, make another. No one likes it when someone bolts and leaves the job for someone else.

- In cube farms, sound travels further than you can imagine; the fabric walls do not always absorb sound effectively, especially if you're trying to concentrate. Be considerate of the nearby cube-dwellers in these areas and move extended conversations to a conference room or some other area away from the masses. Remember also that your cubicle isn't the place to have long meetings. Short discussions to clarify issues are one thing; project updates, design reviews, lengthy tutorials, etc., are another.

- When you pass through a door and another person is coming towards you or behind you, hold the door for them, regardless of their gender and even if they don't thank you for doing so. Why? Because it's the polite thing to do, and the world needs kind and polite people. You're safe if you limit this courtesy to people within ten feet of you. If they're farther than that, let the door close, unless you really want to talk to them or they are carrying something bulky.

- Watch your food in the community refrigerator, and clean up any food explosions in the microwave that you're responsible for. I can tell you with absolute certainty that some of your colleagues will not show the same courtesy. I remember an occasion when someone on the floor of my building transferred to a job in a different location but left her food in her personal fridge. After a couple days the smell was so horrific we called in the building safety person. There was a copier/printer at that end of the hall that got a long rest. I shudder as I write about this incident; I think I can still smell it.

- I've seen an inordinate number of people, during a hallway conversation, lean with their backs on the wall and then place the soles of their shoes on the wall to achieve some kind of three-point stability. Of course, as you can imagine, I find this patently offensive because they probably don't do this in their homes. The point is to treat your workplace with respect.

In any organization you settle in, there will be both celebratory and sad events. Someone is getting married, having a baby, leaving for another job, retiring, or lost a parent, spouse, or other loved one. The correct and proper way to handle these situations is to say *something* to the person involved. Not saying anything is never correct. But there is no need to be long-winded or negative. When someone experiences a death in their family, even if you never got along with them, extend your hand and say *"My condolences on the loss of your mother."* When my father passed away, coming back to work was tough. Nearly everyone said to me what I've written here and close friends spoke to me about his demise in more detail. Approach the person promptly; don't wait a couple of days. I assure you that it means a lot because you heal through the kind thoughts of other people. It's a way of saying "You're not alone with this tragedy." While some people stay home for the permitted mourning period, others may, surprisingly, return to work very soon. They may seek solace at work after tragic events because that is where they spend the majority of their time and it is a familiar place where they feel comfortable and secure. Divorces happen frequently, too. If your colleague's desk is suddenly void of pictures of his wife, don't ask *"So what happened to Marge?"* If a woman you work with suddenly changes her name, she may have recently divorced, not married, so ask around before you rush to offer her congratulations.

The same goes with births and engagements. The engaged couple are excited and you should not rain on their parade by quoting divorce statistics or mentioning how expensive it is to raise children. When I announced to my workgroup that my then fiancée and I were getting married, I received many hearty congratulations. One or two know-it-alls were adamantly advising us on the particulars of our wedding. My point here is that there is no need for you to offer an opinion on how, why, when, where, or what a couple's wedding plans are unless you'll be footing the bill.

For births, deaths, leaving the organization, and marriages there might be a collection to send flowers and a card to sign for the occasion. If you know the person, donate a few dollars; someday, you'll be getting married or having a child, and there may be sad times in your life when flowers from your colleagues or a contribution to a charity might be very important to you. I draw the line at sales for candy that benefit clubs that the children of colleagues belong to. The items for sale are left out with an envelope to deposit the money. I don't feel obligated to support every child's soccer team, church, Cub Scout troop, or youth organization by purchasing overpriced and stale popcorn, magazines, or even worse, mammoth candy bars—especially now that I've improved my cholesterol numbers. The same thing goes for charitable organizations. Give if *you* want to but never feel pressured to give.

It can take some time for people to warm up to you. As a new addition to an already established workgroup you are seen as an outsider and people can be—but won't necessarily be—distant for some period of time. It's a lot like a schoolyard playground, but everyone is older. Be patient, open to invitations to join others for lunch, but not overly friendly.

You sicko, you

You were given sick days for a reason and if you're ill, you should use them. No one wants to be infected with your cold. And the tough trooper attitude does nothing for you, because your productivity has taken a nosedive and that of people you infect will too. So stay home! A day or two spent in bed will do wonders for healing what ails you, and your colleagues will thank you. You won't be awarded a medal for diligence if you come to work coughing, sneezing, feverish and oozing.

Devotion

Religion, like politics is a touchy subject. Whatever your beliefs are—or aren't—remember that it's your choice.

I think the best approach regarding religion is to respect everyone, whatever their beliefs or even if they haven't any formal beliefs. I'm not saying to not answer questions about your belief if someone asks you. And I'm not saying that you shouldn't have religious artifacts at your desk, or read whatever document is sacred to your beliefs during your lunch hour. Show respect for everyone, even if they don't show it back.

I've had to deal with this in light of scandalous criminal behavior by some of the clergy in my religion. The usual comments were "Why would you want to stay a [insert religion here] with all the [insert scandal here] by the [insert name of clergy here]?" Dealing with this type of confrontational behavior isn't easy—aggravation never is. However, in some instances, these comments are made by ignoramuses just to aggravate you, and are best dealt with by removing yourself from the situation—just walk away. If you can't, say quietly and firmly, looking straight into their eyes, that you don't feel it necessary to justify your beliefs to them. Then walk away. You can mention to them that you do not consider their inquiries appropriate and tell them to refrain from future comments on that matter. Suggesting they partake in an impossible solo reproductive act isn't recommended. Prove yourself to be the adult in the room.

It's a good policy to be aware and very sensitive to people's devotion or their sense of propriety. Making fun of or being cynical of others' beliefs or telling libidinous stories to shock a more conservative person is unprofessional conduct. Before you suggest that they can just leave the room if they don't like what you're saying, or that the first amendment protects your right to free speech, remember that the *HR folks will likely side with the person being offended*. There are numerous ways to justify each person's viewpoint, but I urge you to just be ultra-sensitive to the people around you. It's entirely possible that in a select group of people, if you even laughed at an off-color joke, not told it, you could be called on the carpet.

You should respect peoples' temperaments also. Don't deliberately bring up a controversial topic just to see a "high reactor" type of person become riled up.

Your friendship or kinship with a person of a race or ethnicity different from yours does not give you a license to refer to them with a slang term.

Flaming emails

While computers have enabled tremendous increases in our productivity, email has made communication almost *too* easy. When

I neglected to include a key person on the distribution of some data I was sharing (an honest mistake), the person I didn't include, once he discovered my omission, sent me a scathing email and cc'ed the original distribution! I quickly replied to him and to everyone the initial note was sent to and apologized for my mistake, assured him that it was not intentional, and requested that he overlook my honest error. It made him look like a hothead who overreacted. Which is precisely what he was. I've also sent the terse, angry email and felt like a complete idiot thirty seconds after it was on its way. This is something to avoid. Even if the people you fire at are at your level, knee-jerk responses, depending on who they're sent to, contribute to your reputation. If you're upset at someone or something, never send an email while you're still stewing about the issue. You can write the email, but *don't click "send"*. Keep it as a draft. Writing it can help you feel better because it forces you to think the issue through and help you understand the magnitude of your reaction and in a way, help you safely vent your frustration or anger. After you have calmed down, re-read the note you initially wrote and compose a document with a calmer tone.

Your email address at work shouldn't be used for personal matters. Use a Gmail, Yahoo!, or other account for your personal email. Still, remember, everything is monitored so be prudent. If the company doesn't allow surfing the Internet even during lunch hours, don't do it. There are a lot of rules that aren't routinely enforced—until the company decides to.

It's fair to say that viewing, sending or receiving pornography (except if you or your company are a part of the, ah, industry) is never tolerated. I know of a situation where someone was severely reprimanded because he received an inappropriate image on his computer, opened it, recognized it as pornographic, deleted it, but did not report the sender to the corporate office responsible for policing that kind of matter.

This is all a from the way things were years ago. Pornography was a staple in most industrial areas that were populated mainly by men. You would open a tool cabinet and there would be a picture of a young woman with most of her clothes missing. When a woman passed through a shop, the guys would essentially stop working and blatantly stare. Women were treated in condescending fashion, and the glass ceiling that many women speak of was actually reinforced concrete. Women had to tolerate being treated like second-class citizens or leave. And don't even think of the racial imbalance and prejudice. It was so patently obvious, "we'll-hire-who-we-want-never-mind-equality" that you wonder just how backwards-thinking could people be.

Recall that the proper response to "Thank you" is "You're welcome". "No problem" or "Yup" doesn't cut it when someone thanks you for your efforts. Remember to say "Thank you" sometimes even if you're doing the giving.

Expletives and f-bombs

Tempers can flare in the workplace and frustration can become so great that an f-bomb is launched. If I had a nickel for every time I used it, I would, well, have more than a few nickels and this is not something I'm proud of. We (including me) should learn to communicate and articulate our thoughts without using vulgarities to fill the gaps.

Now there are special situations: A fellow I worked with was once employed in a steel mill. He analyzed the steel as it was made and had to communicate his findings to the guys on the floor. He might have been exaggerating, but he said that if every other word wasn't an f-bomb, no one had any idea what he was saying. I'm sure you realize that you probably won't find too many artists and poets on the floor of a steel mill; it's a tough job and sometimes that kind of work brings with it tough language. Not that it's necessary, mind you, but that's the way it is. Military drill sergeants generally don't say "Jeepers-gosh-darn you fellas pretty please stand at attention" when addressing new recruits.

Of even greater importance is to refrain from using profanity when speaking *to a* co-worker, or heaven forbid, your boss. In those instances, the outcome will depend on the person involved.

Company picnics and parties

Before you bring guests to a company event, review the protocol with them. Tell them who's who, who's the big boss, your boss's name, how big your workgroup is, etc. You would hope guests will behave appropriately. They shouldn't trash the company: if the company you work for has an interest someplace that is killing off the purple-tufted frog fly and your guest is an avid environmentalist, request that during the event, they keep a lid on their fervor. They shouldn't pledge undue sincerity to the surly manager whose good graces you're trying to acquire. Insincerity is very easy to detect. It's also important for guests to act and dress appropriately for the type of organization you work in. Occasionally you might be treated to a show at a company event: I attended a holiday party where a couple of the wives of senior level managers went absolutely nuts on the dance floor, hooting and hollering like a bunch of lunatics. We never had an open bar after that.

Chapter 8
You and Your Boss

The world of work can be viewed as having three components: your job, your boss, and the people you work with.

All three are very much intertwined—you can't talk about one without considering the other two. **Be forewarned, though, that my comments will be focused on managing the *negative* aspects of these categories.** No one needs to know how to handle coworkers who are kind and helpful, a boss who's a warm and nurturing leader, or a career that's rewarding and well-paying. It's the jerks who have been sprinkled on this earth that you should know how to deal with. It's the micromanaging, browbeating boss you have to know how to back-manage. And during the periods of frustration that come with every career, you have to know how to stay sane. I'll be drawing on my experiences and how I dealt with them, in addition to my observations and discussions with others.

Before I get too far into the nitty-gritty about bosses, it's important for you to realize what are the characteristics of a good boss or, more appropriately, what should you expect from your boss.

A good boss should:

- Be clear about what he or she expects from you. If you are not meeting his standards, he should promptly discuss his thoughts with you, offer ample time for corrective measures, coach you if necessary, and schedule an improvement plan with reasonable mileposts for you to achieve.

- Be honest and truthful. He shouldn't hide corporate information from you unless it involves future directions of the company that haven't been made public or are otherwise classified.

- Be fair in his dealings with all his subordinates. So another way of saying this is that he shouldn't play favorites. But wait a minute—don't you know people that you like more than others? Sure you do and so will your boss—it's human nature. Your boss will have subordinates that he doesn't care for, but he shouldn't make that known to anyone. The point is that the boss should not take from the people he doesn't like and give to the people he likes. Everyone should be treated the same—given merits— and demerits—based on their performance. Should, however, doesn't always mean will.

- Be available to meet with you and discuss what is on your mind. I've known of bosses who liked to schedule a meeting if you needed to speak to them, and others for whom I could stick my head in their offices and ask if they could talk. If it was going to be a long, involved conversation, I would tell them in advance and ask if they wanted to check their schedule first. Starting a serious, potentially long conversation about your concerns regarding your role in the company's future should be scheduled so that sufficient time can be allotted.

Everybody, including your boss and his boss, has a boss. There is a definite care and feeding protocol of a boss, much like that for owning a pet. Much of the time they respond to how *you* manage *them*. Unfortunately, once in a while you can discover that your boss is rabid or has mistaken you for a fire hydrant or scratching post. And you can't retaliate with a rolled up newspaper. I've had many,

many bosses; most of them good, several excellent, and a couple very, very poor—which I believe is probably not too far removed from what many people experience over the course of their careers.

Bosses are easy targets and, as you know, are frequently fodder for comic strips and TV situational comedies. Everybody laughs, because as I just said—everybody has a boss and the writers or cartoonists craftily blend a little bit of every boss—maybe even theirs—into the character they've created.

I think most people *want* to have a good relationship with their bosses. It makes sense, of course, since your boss will be involved in crafting your performance appraisal which is a critical element of your work history, and will influence your future within the organization. One thing to remember on the subject of bosses is that your boss may not agree with you on many issues. Your boss may have feelings exactly opposite to yours on an issue that you feel deeply passionate about. We all pick our friends because we share some sort of common bond or interest. With a boss and coworkers, you are issued one of the former and many of the latter—there is initially nothing for you to choose. The company essentially says "You're hired. Here's your boss and there are your colleagues. Good luck and get to work." So you have to work with the boss and colleagues who came with your job.

A concept that can be difficult to accept is that a boss who possesses many negative aspects but who delivers what he is supposed to and makes money for the company will be given more latitude than the opposite. His shortcomings will be excused and forgiven until he steps way over a line in the sand that someone has drawn or someone pursues legal action (and their own career suicide) against him.

Speak respectfully to your boss and ignore what anyone else says about him or her, or for that matter, what you think. This isn't being insincere—it's deciding for yourself what kind of person he is. In fact, at one point in my career, I had people offering me prayers and comments like "You poor bastard" when they learned who I was working for. Although the comments made me wary, I wanted to find out for myself what type of fellow he was. So I responded by saying "I'm sorry you feel like that" and wondered if perhaps they were the cause of the negative feelings. It took many years, but I realized that their original sentiments weren't too far off the mark.

Whatever your boss is or isn't, the following items remain clear:

- He is still the boss.

- He can have considerable effect on your career. Don't fear him and don't worship him; just remember that he has his job for a reason. Even if everyone around believes that your boss shouldn't be in his position, someone in the organization, likely your boss's superior, believes differently. He may think very highly of him and listen very carefully to what he says: about *you, your* project, *your* potential as an employee, the expensive equipment *you* need to do *your* job or the meeting you want to attend in Florida held in the middle of winter. He probably has known your boss for quite some time while *you,* as the new person, are a complete stranger with no credibility. Your boss could have been recently promoted to his position and still be learning.

- Remember when dealing with your boss that there's a big difference between disagreeing and being disagreeable. Disagreeing is a difference of opinion. Being disagreeable is being a pain in the ass about the disagreement.

- Incompetent bosses will ultimately be discovered, but if they're crafty enough, it may take a while. Think in terms of years, if it ever happens.

- Trying to discredit or get your boss fired is a waste of your time; if you really can't stand him or her, find another job.

The many faces of your boss

The relationship between bosses and subordinates is multi-faceted. The boss might have multiple subordinates at different levels, i.e., technician, engineer, project leader, salesperson, marketing coordinator, and administrative assistant. His interaction with each person will be different. You have to create and nurture your relationship with him, with the goal being a reputation as someone who knows what he's doing, shows his best effort, is trustworthy, responsible, and who doesn't cause trouble or brew bad feelings in the group. No one is all of these things all of the time.

Your boss might have some people in his workgroup that he seems to be friendlier with. They may carpool together or be friends from earlier connections in the company. It is important to learn who the boss's friends are and while not letting them step all over you, act on a request from them with a *slight* bit more urgency. Fact: people can speak negatively about others they feel are difficult to deal with.

When you do your work to the best of your ability, you make your boss look good, which puts you in a favorable light in his eyes. You'll be a low-maintenance person and bosses like that because it makes life easy for them. No supervisor desires a subordinate that incites doubt—basic questions like "What he's doing?", or "Does he know what to do and how to do it?" "Is he goofing off and being obvious about it?" "Is he going around saying stupid things and making me look bad?" If you create a mess, sure, you look like a fool, *but so does your boss*. And he won't like that—would you?

Did *I* do that?

Avoidable accidents in your work group can cause your boss to show you a less pleasant side of his personality. I've always worked in a technical work area, where things like fires, explosions, smoke, and other incidents were rare occurrences but not unheard of. I'm at a loss to give many examples but I imagine this can also happen in an office environment—maybe a coffee pot overheats, or an inexperienced person attempts to service the copier or printer and spills toner all over the carpet. Wherever there are human beings, there will be accidents.

True story: At one time, my boss and I completed a technical activity in the lab and then went to another part of the building to attend to another matter. As we were walking back to the lab, I mentioned how upsetting it would be if our previous activity in the lab, as it was electrical in nature, resulted in clouds of smoke when we returned. We both agreed that it wouldn't be a desirable outcome. As we rounded the corner to the lab, we saw, to our horror, that the lab *was* filled with smoke! We immediately shut the apparatus off and my boss had the presence of mind to open an exhaust duct that quickly vented the smoke away, and left only a slight residual odor of which we claimed ignorance when anyone asked. ("You smell something? I don't smell anything! Everything is fine. No problem at all.") The rest of the day was uneventful, and to this day only he and I knew of this occurrence. The smoke came from the device warming up the first time it was used, so we decided to stick around the next time we did that sort of procedure. But we were relieved not to have an unusual incident broadcast through the entire building.

Although bosses realize that accidents happen, they, as well as you, do not appreciate special attention from unusual incidents, especially if they result in smoke, fire, streams of water or any other chemical, or evacuating the building. You are better off not seeing safety personnel, fire marshals, and workplace facilities managers.

Incidentally, if the safety or fire marshals show up, as they might do for building inspections, and are perusing your work area, greet them enthusiastically; ask them to please look around and offer suggestions. This will throw them way off guard. Most people are not happy to see them because they represent authority and regulations, and they have some power. But if you welcome them you are much better off because you are showing intent to do the right thing. If you are close to creating a disaster, it's easier to say "I'm so happy I invited you into my area so that you could discover the potential problem." Isn't this just a cover-your-behind tactic? Yes, it is.

George Bernard Shaw said the following regarding mistakes:
"A life spent making mistakes is not only more honorable
but more useful than a life spent doing nothing."

For the majority of the mistakes you make at work, you can redeem yourself. The key is to be first off the blocks, so to speak, to acknowledge and apologize. Be the first to admit the mistake you made, and don't follow it up with an excuse, rationalization, redirected blame, or any falsehoods.

Feeding your boss's inner beast

At the beginning of this chapter I compared a boss to a pet. Continuing with that metaphor, keep your boss well-fed. And what do bosses feed on? Progress, be it data, plans, reports—all the stuff that's called work. Many bosses adhere to the MBWA method: Management By Walking Around. Your work group may be scattered in different areas or labs in the building, and managers like to check on everyone a couple times a day. My colleagues and I referred to it as a "bed check." The boss needs to see you working on your assigned tasks, and wants to hear if you have any problems or issues for him to resolve. Like the owner of a pet dog, have "treats" for your boss at these times, nuggets of information, so when he saunters up and asks "So how are things going?" or "Have you made any progress on the competitive analysis of our flange hole patterns?" you can satisfy their craving for information. You don't have to feed them every time you see them because they understand that work can be in progress and that you either are getting things done or have recently completed something, and are digesting the outcome by graphing the data, checking the code for bugs, or reviewing the client list or marketing plan. He may have something else on his mind, be on his way to some meeting, or for any of a million other reasons not want to stop and chat with you right at that moment. Let him run free, but when he comes to you, have something for him. A good friend and colleague of mine introduced me to the concept of having "treats" for your boss. We both used it effectively for many years.

By keeping your boss fed, you are building his confidence in you, and over time his visits will become less frequent. He will know that you're consistently on top of things. You have established a positive *work ethic* (or at least the appearance of one.) The work report "treats" you provide him better be actual, not filler material. They will always see bullshit for what it is.

Appearances and impressions

Consider this scenario: You have been working steadily for several hours and need to clear your mind, so you visit a site on the internet to check on your sports team or the news and weather. Your boss unexpectedly stops into your work area to discuss something with you, sees what's on your screen, doesn't say anything, talks with you about what he wants, and then goes back to his office. Feeling refreshed after your internet diversion, you go back to work.

Several hours pass and you take another break on an Internet site or play some game on your phone. Again your boss walks in and sees you on the Internet or staring at your phone. He speaks to you about what he came to see you for, goes back to his office, and you go back to work.

On another day you decide to share a cup of coffee with a colleague and discuss your plans for the weekend. Your boss stops by your cube to speak to you and seeing you absent, heads somewhere else, but passes by the break room where you are obviously having a leisurely conversation.

Sometimes a boss can take several instances like those I've described, and combine them with the pressure *his* boss is putting on him to increase his groups productivity, his own personal problems, or his own inability to understand the dynamics of the workplace. Now perhaps you mention that you are going to be late with a task (maybe through no fault of your own) and he spouts off that he's not surprised, because every time he sees you, "…you're surfing the net or having coffee."

Is he right? The correct answer is "It depends." What does it depend on?

- Whether your deliverables are usually on time.
- Whether he knows the reason you are going to be late in this instance is not due to these micro-breaks you take.
- Whether he is even thinks beyond what he has seen. This relates to his overall intelligence.
- Whether you and he get along.

You might say that the boss who I've described above is more like a bodily orifice reserved for the elimination of metabolic waste. While this may be correct, the fact remains he has labeled you as a goof-off.

You have to understand that what your boss sees, and other aspects of your relationship with him, feed into the impression he has of you. This is why people don't like having their computer screens visible to everyone: Many people use the Internet as a momentary diversion from their assigned work and none of them want to be caught. There are a brave few that don't care either way.

The point is to assess your boss: is he/she a hard-driving, workaholic with no sense of humor and who offers no glimpse of his/her life outside of work? If so, then don't get caught—and the best way to avoid detection is not to do anything in the first place. If you need a break, step away from your desk for a few minutes and walk to another part of the building, visit the restroom and wash your face to refresh yourself or turn away from your computer monitor and focus on something else in your work area. Check your phone away from your desk.

If you feel that your boss would not mind an occasional diversion, you can trust your feeling. But if, or more likely when, you are caught, don't hide anything or make a hurried attempt to "x" out of where you are or use a keyboard shortcut to do the same. Ask him directly: *"I wanted to take a break for a few minutes and visit [your diversion site, as long as it's not inappropriate]—is that ok with you?"* Whatever the answer is, you will know where he stands on that issue.

It's not unreasonable to expect some interim performance feedback six months after starting a job. After that amount of time, it's good to reflect and take stock of where you are. Request some time on his schedule so you don't catch him off guard, but don't schedule it in the middle of a business crisis. Pose the questions

"How am I doing?" "Am I doing what I should be doing?" "Do you have any constructive criticism to offer me at this point?" This kind of question can help initiate helpful discussions. *"Are you pleased with my performance on this job so far?"* Without putting a sharp point on it, mention to your boss that you would like to address any issues he has with your work as soon as possible, **not** at your annual performance appraisal. I've told bosses of mine that if they want me to do something different, or if they see something that they do not like, tell me and I'll immediately implement a change, as I do not want any surprises down the road. Incidentally, if there is some facet of work that concerns you don't say *"I'm worried about."* You're *concerned* about the issue, whatever it is – *never worried.* *Worried* conveys a free-floating, hand-wringing anxiety about a problem. The word *concerned* conveys recognition of a problem that has the potential to reflect poorly on the organization. It's a subtle difference.

©2011 King Features Syndicate, Inc. World Rights Reserved.

As a new employee, if your boss has some criticism about your performance, take heart in the fact that you probably do have a lot to learn. You're new to the job, the working world, the company, and so on. He probably doesn't expect you to be perfect. If you were an overall poor performer, *he* would start the discussion. In any event, *listen carefully,* with your mouth shut, to what your boss has to say. When he's finished, don't become defensive. Take heart in knowing that your boss has given you some feedback. There are some, probably too many, dysfunctional bosses who don't communicate at all until they begin erupting like Mount St. Helens.

What should you do if Mr. Vesuvius calls you into his office and "rips you a new one"? You could say *"OK. I've heard what you said."* And then say *"I need some time to digest what you've told me. I will probably have some questions or need to clarify some issues so I expect that we can talk again."* Go away, calm down, and think about everything — point by point — your boss said. Try to write it down. Digest it all. If he misunderstood something you've done, or your intent, or missed some extenuating circumstances, the second meeting with him is where you present your side of the story. Maybe he's right — you're not showing enough initiative, or are arriving late, or not punctual with reports – whatever. You may have your reasons but clearly you have to meet his expectations of you.

In the second meeting *clarify* what he said. Say that you want to play it back to him to make sure you understand it. *Acknowledge* your error or shortcoming and if applicable, *present* your side of the story. This is the time for you to present any extenuating circumstances that contributed to the issue. Next, *conceive* a plan to satisfy his expectations. He may use the Nike approach: "Just do it." If so, then just promise to do your best but request some periodic feedback so you know you are giving him what he wants.

I had a boss who misinterpreted my explanations of how I handled problems and claimed I was being defensive. Situations with people like this are not easy to resolve. If the manager doesn't look inward and ask what he can do to help his under-performing subordinate, it's up to the employee to find some path to meeting his boss's performance requirements, and he may not know exactly *what* he needs. My boss probably wanted me to say *"Yes boss, I have failed and will try and do better,"* but it's not all that simple, as you may need something from your boss in order to perform better. If your boss throws the defensive flag on you, backtrack and make sure he realizes that you are not deflecting any blame, even though you may not deserve any. Accept *some* of the blame, but *request his help* in order to improve your performance. Depending on the situation, additional training or coaching may be necessary.

The compliment sandwich

It is common that companies formally assess your performance on a yearly basis. In these performance reviews, which should be written and signed by both you and your boss, you may see suggestions of "things to work on" compiled in what I refer to as the *compliment sandwich*. This is a less-than-positive comment with one or more positive comments on either side. It's a palliative technique for delivering negative feedback. When you take a bite of the sandwich, the negative part is a smaller percentage—but it's still negative and still there. Managers include them in performance feedbacks so the employee has something to work on but they don't want to put too sharp a point on it. For example, consider the following fictional words:

"Roscoe had a good first year in his position as a sales engineer. He completed the company's training on schedule and shadowed two senior level sales engineers for six months each. His telephone conversations with potential customers were handled well and as thoroughly as he was able. The information and solutions he quickly recommended to people only occasionally needed to be corrected or revised.

During his second year, Roscoe should focus on accurately aligning customer's request to our available product line. He should understand that it is acceptable to delay his response to requests so that he can be sure of the information he is delivering. He should realize it is quite acceptable to delay, rather than to have to call back a customer and rescind a hasty response.

As his supervisor, I note and applaud his friendly but business-like attitude and his ability to engage with his co-workers. He will continue to be an asset to our team and I look forward to working with him in the future."

The italicized section, while not negative, implies that in order to complete inquiries quickly, Roscoe would sometimes give incorrect information and then have to call the customer and correct his recommendation. This is not unexpected in a new employee, and is noted in the first section as occurring "only occasionally." His supervisor is telling him to take more time to answer inquiries, so that he gets it right the first time. It can be called a "less than positive" remark that is something for him to work on. Since I've created this fictional person as a good, earnest employee, I would expect that Roscoe's review after his second year would likely highlight that he took the "meat" from the sandwich to heart and his boss perhaps said that he was "quickly becoming an expert on several challenging applications, and is sought out by his colleagues for his opinion."

I point out this easily-overlooked detail in a performance appraisal so that you will take advantage of it to further enhance your performance and value as an employee.

By the way, you should know that signing your performance assessment doesn't necessarily mean you agree to what is written, just that you've seen it. It's also a good idea to get copies of the signed document and store a second copy in your home office.

A primer on difficult bosses

From what I've seen and experienced, many problems with bosses seem to involve control issues. On one hand, bosses want their people to have control over their jobs and feel empowered, but on the other hand, they don't want them to have too much control because then the boss doesn't feel like a boss anymore. It's as if some bosses want to be the school crossing guard: "Go ahead and move, but only when I say so and tell you where." As a boss, it seems they want to control.

A boss who insists on micro-managing his people is a good example of someone with a control issue. This type of person may insist on being involved at every step. They don't necessarily criticize what you do, but check to see if you did it. You earn points if you did it in the manner they would have. Sometimes a micro-manager is also a perfectionist. He will both check and either correct or rephrase memos that you write which is known to drive whole populations of employees mad.

It is possible that these types of managers are just missing the action; they're stuck doing manager stuff and miss the hands-on work. Other times, it's just the way they are, so let him/her look over your shoulder. If you're doing your job, you should have nothing to hide. It's about control, so fighting it, arguing with him, or begging him for a longer leash will be fruitless.

Eventually he may drive himself out of the world of management, but that is his problem. Let him check and verify. Why create an adversary when you can foster the relationship and put someone in your corner? Why do you have to put up with his management style? Because he's the boss. If he delivers what he's supposed to in an acceptable timeframe and within the budget, his eccentricity is will not only be tolerated, but rewarded. Results are what count.

Mr. Perfect

Perfectionists are difficult—no—make that *impossible* to please, unless you do things exactly their way. And by exact I mean you have to be a clone of them. By the way, you will never be able to do things exactly their way. A key point for survival is, again, to relinquish control. Instead of praying they get struck by lightning, a useful tactic is to learn from this person when he begins to dissect your way of doing something. Ask why he wants things done a certain way in a "I-just-want-to-learn" manner. His way may be better. If you learn what he wants and give it to him before he asks for it, you have started writing your ticket to freedom. In time he will put slack in your line. And it may be on a geological time frame.

I once worked for a perfectionist, and it isn't something I want to do again. The position was in a lab where everyone had their own bench at which to work. Mine was situated so that my back was to the entrance to the room. A coworker of mine told me that my boss would frequently quietly walk up and stand behind me as I worked at my bench, and "eyeball" me—follow me with just his eyes—watch me work—and then just as quietly return to his office. I found it kind of creepy when my colleague told me about it. I never confronted my boss but I wondered what he was looking for.

My difficulty with this boss was pretty much common knowledge; one of my colleagues capitalized on this one day. She came into the lab all excited and smiling and said to me:

"Frank! Guess who's leaving the lab and moving out of state?"

With unbounded joy I said *"Seymour?"* (my boss)

She said *"YES!"*

I said *"You're kidding!"* with my faith in justice restored.

She replied *"YES, I am!"* and then had a good laugh, while my spirits nosedived and I wondered if NASA needed someone to staff a mission to another planet.

I didn't handle my relationship with the perfectionist very well. I fought, resisted, and clearly wasn't perfect like him. One week after a big blow-up, where everyone else could hear us yelling at each other through the closed door to his office, I had an interview which resulted in the second contract job I had, which after a year and a half, led to my most lengthy, multi-decade career.

Why did I fail at this relationship? Why did I do the wrong things? Well, for starters, there wasn't a document like the one you're holding. And there was room for additional tolerance on my part. I didn't like the job from the start—this was the job in the governmental agency I told you about in an earlier chapter. So I left for other, hopefully greener, pastures. When I announced this to my boss, he wished me well, and said he hoped that, despite our differences, I would think well of him in future years. And honestly, I have and still do. In fact, I've remembered and used many of the things he told me. Being who I am, I was almost destined to return to the industrial world. Hindsight being always 20/20, I shouldn't have taken the job. But we all make mistakes.

The big mistake I made was participating in the loud argument. I should have just listened to him and not given it back to him. I was fortunate that I was determined not to stay in that organization for much longer. Even after the first week I thought about leaving. If it were an organization where I wanted to stay, I would have had a black mark or blemish on my reputation. Everyone would remember "...the day when Frank and Seymour went at each other big time."

Tyrannosaurus boss

The famous football coach Vince Lombardi is quoted as having said *"If you aren't fired with enthusiasm, you will be fired [dismissed from your job] with enthusiasm."* That certainly is a clear message as to what he expected from his subordinates.

I knew of another manager who was fond of delivering what he called *attitude* enemas to subordinates who fell from his favor, during which he would loudly dress you down and cover all of the faults and shortcomings he thought you had. Unfortunately, the screaming lunatic approach isn't the way things are done these days, thank heavens. Fortunately, for me I've never had a boss like this, but I've been able to observe while others have been subjected to one. I know a very bright young man who worked for this type of person. During a staff meeting he dozed off, or as I like to say, "Had some long blinks."

Staff meetings can frequently be dull, and if you are drowsy for one reason or another, you can be sucked into dreamland against your wishes. After the meeting, the boss called him aside and spent more than a few minutes berating him for the time he spent with Mr. Sandman. What the boss should have done was call him aside, put a hand on his shoulder, and ask him, in a serious but fatherly way, if he was feeling OK. Or he could have done the stern-but-fair manager routine. This lets the fellow know that his lethargy was apparent and gives him an out—he can mumble something about not feeling up to par and then be more alert in future meetings. But to berate someone, even in private, is not the correct approach. It creates bad feelings all around. The worst case is if the boss mentions it on his subordinate's performance appraisal. Then it's in writing and virtually impossible to delete, so your only option is to earn more performance appraisals with positive feedback after the appraisal with the negative comment. Although it can take years, because performance reviews usually take place once a year, sustained above-average performance dilutes an earlier negative glitch. A believable excuse, such as working for someone known as being not easy to work for, is also a suitable diluent for negative comments.

It's too bad you weren't forewarned from the interview, but everyone (including you) is on their best behavior. Even if you had some inklings of it, you, like me, were trying to decide for yourself or perhaps thought that he was just nervous, or that he couldn't *really* be that way. People can be just about any way you can imagine. If you have been sexually harassed, emotionally and/ or verbally harassed, physically assaulted, or threatened you should wake up the Human Resources people. They will take those types of situations very seriously; you can't recall them once you start that particular ball rolling so be prepared to go the distance. You cannot change your mind if you begin to file a complaint with them. Once they get the scent of something potentially illegal or off-policy, they will hunt it down like a dog so be prepared to follow it to the end.

Verbal harassment can be filled with fine lines. For example, if your boss says that some error you made was "a stupid mistake" it *might* not be considered verbal harassment depending on where it was said. It he said it in an auditorium filled with people who chuckled at it or shook their heads, in my opinion (as a legal *non*-professional) it was certainly in bad taste and he should at least be at least be reprimanded. If the two of you were alone or with a third person and it was more of a smart-aleck comment that did not diminish your reputation in front of many people, then you might have to let it pass. Or you might inquire if he ever recently admitted or experienced the personal tragedy of making an error (thick sarcasm intended). Sometimes you have to seize the opportunity to gently nudge the boss away from "that line" he is approaching. I can't elaborate on every circumstance, but advise you to talk it over with a friend or colleague before you seek retribution.

A minimally-organized boss

A disorganized boss can be worse than one who maintains tight, inflexible, control, because he will put minimal thought into his decisions. Everything that he demands will also be last-minute, since he is too disorganized to put enough thought into his plan.

If you are assigned a task that appears to be a waste of your effort, doing what is asked of you is a safe action. Perhaps you don't fully understand or your boss hasn't fully explained the situation. Remember that he is still the boss.

The pacifist

A boss can be uncomfortable confronting a subordinate about a performance or behavioral issue. It is the boss's job to handle problems, but if he is hesitant to get involved, document what's going on and provide him the information through emails to insure that he can't feign ignorance. The same tactic applies if the boss is unable to make a decision. Keep him informed that the issue has not gone away and still needs his attention. If he passes the buck to a subordinate (like you, for instance), emails detailing your rationale for making your decision are critically important, and should also include the fact that the responsibility of making a decision was delegated to you by your boss. This is often referred to as *covering your ass*. It needs to be covered in case someone wants an ass to chew out—and you don't want it to be yours.

For conflict issues with your boss that you feel compelled not to dismiss, find out if there is an *ombudsman* at the company to discuss the problem with. They are allegedly impartial and will keep conversations confidential. Ask them *before you speak with them* about the confidentially of what you discuss with them. If they respond that it is up to their discretion, say thank you, leave, and consider discussing it with someone else, either in your group (a more senior person) or a friend or family member. Select someone who will be objective and as impartial as possible.

Exploring your options

When you are at the breaking point with your boss, the obvious options are either staying or leaving your workgroup for one that has a more pleasant environment. Here are a few points to consider before you make your decision:

- As a relatively new hire, you might be required to stay for some length of time in your group. Companies can't allow employees to jump quickly from place to place. You have to stay and deal with it in some fashion or resign from the company which is something you should not consider unless 1) the situation is completely intolerable 2) you have exhausted all efforts to resolve the problem or 3) you have another offer in hand. Like a marriage, a commitment to work at a company can be annulled. More about this later.

- The boss may be having some personal problems: death of a loved one, divorce, health issues, child rearing issues, work pressures (maybe his boss is causing *him* some grief), etc. You probably won't know this immediately, so cut him some slack initially. If he's riding you about some issue, you can tell him that you realize this is an important issue and that you will do your best to not let him down.

- The wonderful-appearing boss in an adjacent department whom you feel would be an improvement over your current situation can turn out to be much worse! People have different "faces" — and the face that Mr. Wonderful shows you might not be the one you see if you work for him. It's even possible that you could have a deeper conflict with a new boss. Your approach should be slow and careful. "Better the devil you know than the one you don't."

- You can bide your time and wait for upper management to realize he might be a loose cannon, though if this ever happens, it could take *years*. If the boss acts this way and the company has *confidential* surveys where they try to find out what's important to the employees, you can offer feedback. Maybe you feel that you should just slam him and give back to him what he gave out, but if you do, *you* shouldn't come across as a lunatic. Just state that "…as a subordinate to Seymour, ", you and your colleagues "have been the brunt of numerous" and then mention his particular shortcoming. Ranting on and on can be tossed out as oddball comments. "I would like to make management aware of this behavior hoping that they initiate corrective action before it escalates to litigious levels."

- If you've witnessed your boss being difficult with your colleagues, but you and he have a good relationship, remember that it's their problem, not yours, so stay out of it. Your colleagues may have brought this on themselves. And you now know his hot button. You are, however, a witness, should legal action be taken if, for example, you saw the boss act inappropriately to one of your colleagues. Make sure that they aren't dating, though.

- If your boss doesn't bring it up, you can make a specific problem you're having with him a topic for discussion at your annual or interim review. Be gentle, but perfectly clear. For example if you feel you are continually being burdened with an unfavorable task you can say, "I've done the last six flange inventories. I realize its importance, but it requires spending three days in the dusty warehouse which is sweltering in the summer and frigid in the winter. Can this task be shared among the whole group?" Your boss might see your request as reasonable and act accordingly. But what if he says that this is a task that is usually done by the new hires in the group?

- Ask him why, but don't be confrontational and don't give him an "out." If you say to him "Do you feel that this task is an excellent way for new employees to learn the flange product line?" he might say "Yeah, sure, that's the reason!" because it's an easy answer, can be construed as reasonable, and he doesn't have to think. If, however, he says that you seem to complete it so quickly and accurately, you can suggest that with some assistance it could be completed even sooner. A key word here is to *brainstorm* some resolution.

- If he ends the discussion, attempt to discuss the situation with a colleague you feel comfortable with, preferably one with more years with the company.

- If it seems that you're being singled out, attempt to discuss it with your boss's boss. But be very careful here. You are dancing on quicksand. Make this the absolute last tactic you use, and have an exit plan to another job, as this can create bad feeling between you and your immediate boss.

- Prepare yourself for the cold front that will make its way into your work life.
- Recall the Chinese proverb "Before seeking revenge, first dig two graves."

A few more thoughts on an over-controlling boss:

- Watch how he acts towards other members of your workgroup; perhaps he's being cautious because you're new. You have to build up credibility and trust.
- If you are scheduled to deliver a presentation, discuss it with him beforehand. Ask him point blank if he plans on letting you speak the entire time. Propose to him that if he has something crucial to say he wait until you're finished unless if you've made a serious error. You can propose that if you've been asked a question out of your realm of experience or that you find difficult, you will direct the question to him. For example, if someone asks you what changes you plan to implement in Fabulous Flange's marketing strategy for the following year you can say "I can speak for a few changes but that is best addressed by Seymour." (your boss) I discuss these tactics in the chapter on meetings and presentations.
- Try to find some niche where you can begin to do something on your own. Don't concern yourself if it's not earth-shattering work that will bring you fame, fortune, and promotions. The key element is that it's something you can do without interference from your boss. If he begins to hover around you when you are working on this item, consider asking him if you could show him your progress on a weekly or biweekly schedule.
- Attempt to understand his particular manner of doing things,

and if at all possible, suggest an alternative approach that is more efficient or that significantly improves the process.

- Assert your desire to have more independence eventually. "Eventually" can mean very different things to you and your boss. To you, it could mean a few months, but to your boss, it could mean a year. Credibility is acquired over time by successfully completing assigned tasks and contributing to the work environment.

While you wouldn't be the first person in the world to resign because you hate your boss, try again to deal with your boss and not let him define your destiny. Remember this: as you deal with your boss's idiosyncrasies, so will he deal with yours. If you want your boss to tolerate you when you're not firing on all cylinders, accept him for what he and you both are: imperfect human beings. A positive spin on having a difficult boss is that he can help you develop a thicker skin, which is valuable.

A colleague of mine had the following posted on his desk: "No man is totally worthless; he can always serve as a bad example."

When you ascend the corporate ladder, *you* will be a better boss.

There may be occasions when you need to speak to someone a level higher than your boss but you want or need to avoid passing through the usual chain of command or going through his administrative assistant. I needed to speak to my boss's boss in order to return to my "home" area after being selected for a temporary assignment in another area. I knew the person I needed to speak to fairly well, and since he was in upper management, he had an assigned parking space. We used to arrive at work close to the same time. So one morning I took my time getting out of my car, fumbling with some papers and such until I saw that fellow pull into his parking space. I "happened" to walk into the building with him, chatting about miscellaneous matters before mentioning, almost as an aside, my desire to move back to the area I had previously worked at. I gently, but adamantly, requested the transfer and his assistance if there was any interference. Of course, I had already established an excellent reputation with this fellow so he took my request seriously and after a few more political maneuvers, I went home.

Is this stalking? Not even close, since it was a onetime event. While the commando types would call it *reconnaissance,* it is far from ingenuous. After all, telemarketers call your house when you are most likely to be home. You don't want to make a habit of this, lest your intended subject decides to find other means to get to work or find other ways to avoid you.

Remember this about the HR people, though, should you decide to talk to them about an issue: they work for the same company you do. They will act in the *company's* best interest. They are neither counselors nor a shoulder to cry on. They may be friendly, but they *are not your friends.*

Chapter 9
The People

"A tough lesson in life that one has to learn is that not everybody wishes you well." — Dan Rather

Dan Rather illustrates a harsh reality. The people you work and live with can fall into three very broad, somewhat overlapping, categories: those who want you to succeed, those who don't care one way or the other if you succeed or fail, and lastly, those who want you to fail.

An insightful and poignant quote that has been attributed to the late Maya Angelou is that "People will forget what you said, people will forget what you did, but people will never forget *how you made them feel.*" (italics are mine.) Think about it: how you make people feel touches them at their core. The advice I'm offering is based in many instances on unfavorable situations and try as I might, it is difficult not to see how I felt. While we all remember the good times in our lives, I think a lot of us vividly remember two types of people: Those who hurt our feelings and those who made us feel good about ourselves. Which type do you want to be?

In any subset of the population, be it a company, school, club, religious group, athletic facility—whatever organization you can imagine—you will find people who are

- Kind and understanding
- Generous to a fault
- Helpful team players
- Trustworthy

- Charming and fun-loving with a great sense of humor
- Amazingly brilliant
- Rock solid, salt-of-the-earth types

And you will also become acquainted with people who are

- Obstinate, inflexible, and uncompromising
- Thrifty. Miserly might be a better word.
- Self-centered beyond belief.
- Backstabbing s.o.b.s
- Miserable outwardly and inwardly.
- Dumb as a box of rocks.
- Peculiar. Maybe weird, crazy, or even psychotic by some standards.

Everyone has personal traits that annoy some people and leave others unfazed. It generally takes the confines of a long term marital or committed relationship to be made aware of yours (but that is material for another time).

I'm continually amazed by the diversity of people in the workplace, the manner in which some people can be so *different*. For example, one morning my coworkers and I were sipping our coffee before heading off to our respective work areas. As we chatted about work and personal matters, we could see people through a nearby window as they came from the parking lot into the building. One fellow came into view as he trudged his way towards us: He had a briefcase in one hand, a laptop bag in the other, and a ring-like object around his neck. As he neared closer, one of us said "Is that a toilet seat around his neck?" It was. We were hysterical, and came to find out that the poor fellow had some problems with his backside and needed a doughnut-like support to tolerate sitting at his desk. Anyone else on the planet would put it in a bag or carry it under their arm, but not this fellow—"…it's all about being efficient", he probably thought, "...never mind how foolish I look." I still laugh and shake my head when I think about it.

A major component of your job is the other individuals who make up your department or work area. Like the previous chapter on bosses, dealing with some aspects of the people might be challenging.

They're just like you, only different

Remember that your colleagues may be very different from the friends you had in school.

The differences can be unique religious beliefs, multiple marriages (not just two or three, but five or six), bizarre personality quirks or personal habits, interests that border on the unusual, or interests dramatically different from yours. Some of the people at work will be your parents' age and others even younger than you.

For example, in an organization I was hired into, there were many men who were absolutely enthralled with trains. Toy trains, real trains, pictures of trains, books about trains—these guys loved 'em all, which I thought was a bit "different" for adult men.

Your coworkers might not initially be as open as your friends in school were. After all, in school you all started at about the same time, but at work, you are the new guy and they have to get to know you. Some may appear quite odd but be highly regarded in the organization. It will be a melting pot, sometimes with a bit of slag on the top.

The best friendships I have today are with people I met at work. Pleasant relationships with your co-workers are extremely valuable from the point of mental health and productivity. I think it is fair to say that most of us want to be cared about, be it a hearty "Welcome back!" after a vacation, a get-well card in the midst of an illness, or just the daily banter between people. Friendships at work—sometimes referred to as *collegial*—are helpful for getting things done, from problem solving to knowing who to contact for an issue. If follows that the more people you know, the more people will seek you out because even if you don't know how to do something, you will probably know who does.

There are some people who don't seem to care if they are included in the social side of work: they may be shy, introverted, or for whatever reason, keep to themselves—and they are entitled to be that way, of course. There are others who are quite the opposite—you probably know someone like this—and it is their choice to be that way as long as their outgoing personalities don't subtract from the productivity of the workplace. The rest of us fill in the gap between the two extremes.

There are several avenues for you to meet people and make friends at your job. Of course, you will have collaborations on work issues and may eat lunch with your colleagues, but there may be softball and volleyball teams, ski trips, and other company-sponsored events like group picnics and holiday parties. These events give you a chance to see a different (sometimes unpleasant) side of your colleagues and meet their significant others. Some companies employ off-site team-building events to draw everyone together; these can be a lot of fun and beneficial to the team. Generally though, these latter events are meant to supplement the work the group does, so a lot of time is spent on crafting a mission statement or solving a problem, which is meant to create additional cohesion among everyone. Not particularly enjoyable, in my opinion, but play along and they might send in lunch. "Free" food, meaning that you don't have to open your wallet to pay for it, but only be an active participant in a meeting or workshop is frequently used as a motivational tool or method to lessen the pain of a long meeting.

Where the problems start

I think a lot of problems between colleagues stem from the egos of the people involved; usually the ego of one person needs to be frequently reinforced which I believe is seated in his/her insecurities. This may seem a gross generalization, but in my experience, the egos of people played a significant role in many of the problems I knew of first- or second-hand.

Once you understand what can set people off, it is easier to steer clear of that area and it can also facilitate dealing with their issues. Of course, everyone has their peculiarities—maybe they aren't apparent at work—but they are there.

Don't be a doormat, Matt

I've dealt with people who would step over me if I collapsed in the hall, yet when they needed something from me, they couldn't be more charming. I always feel like checking for my wallet and wristwatch after they left. What has made me feel less "used" is requesting something from them that will be of value to me *when I* assist them because I've found them to have many excuses for not helping me otherwise.

Why help them at all? Because you have to, if it's something the organization needs in order to move forward. The fact that they are "not nice" isn't a good reason to not help them. To ensure that the person you will be helping will assist you at some point in the future, you can write a mail note that includes both supervisors. State that you are "assisting Herman by supplying him with sales forecasts and expect that he will, in *the spirit of teamwork,* promptly supply you with (mention something you may need in the future)." By including both supervisors, you have leverage if that individual is slow to deliver, since you can then forward your original note with the agreement. Does this sound childish or nitpicking? It may, depending on what kind of experiences you have had. You may just feel that by helping them you are also helping the company grow, contributing to their "bottom line" or just not wanting to "play politics." That is all well and good, but after you get stung a few times, you might feel differently. If possible, though, attach your name to what is requested of you to illustrate ownership or where the data came from. I stress that you don't have to—and I suggest you don't—expect something in return each time someone asks you for something. I'm describing a tactic for dealing with the people who are always on the receiving end. If you flat out refuse, count on your requester distributing a memo to your respective bosses which makes you look bad. If the type of person who is constantly taking ascends to managerial levels, you are obligated to give him what he wants, when and how he wants it and it's not a bad idea to follow up with him to make sure he's satisfied.

To refuse a reasonable request is pretty much inadvisable, though you can negotiate the time frame if you have conflicting issues.

If he's requesting action in an unreasonable timeframe, mention the problem to him in an email *in the most non-accusatory manner possible*. For example, you can say "Getting the information you requested may take some additional time due to the other deliverables I have. Can you give me some leeway or ask Boris (your boss) to re-prioritize them so that I can act on this [the current] request?" Make sure that he confirms what he wants from you. Sometimes, this may make him pause and re-think his request. If that doesn't work, you can involve your manager.

I worked with a fellow who was obsessed with mentioning how early he arrived at work each day. If he ever stopped in on a weekend, it seemed that he expected it to be broadcast over the public address system. Yes, he did consistently come in at least an hour early during the regular workweek, but he would spend this hour surfing the internet, making coffee, and doing tasks that were non-essential to his assigned project. His workday ended an hour before everyone else's so he wasn't burning the candle at both ends. What this fellow didn't quite understand is that *results count and appearances don't (as much)*. In addition, *planning* to do something is not worthy of mentioning until it is completed. I like the succinctness of this quote: *"Never confuse movement with action."* – Ernest Hemingway

---

Marion Al Gause, Sr., the late father of my friends Kala, Richard, and Chris Gause, had some wonderful advice for his children: *"Work for a cause, not for applause. Live life to express, not impress. One doesn't have to strive to make his presence noticed when his absence will be felt."* So keeping with Mr. Gause's wisdom, don't attempt to impress your colleagues with your efforts, nor be impressed when a coworker parades his/her efforts for all to see. Everyone works hard, or is supposed to, or at least act like they are.

It's fine to say "I'm swamped!" when you are very busy and someone asks you how things are going but don't exaggerate your workload or diligence.

A good boss will acknowledge, especially in an employee's performance appraisal, any ongoing extra efforts they made or conscientiousness that went above and beyond the norm. Cash might be given to an employee or team who has delivered way beyond expectations. Money has a way of making the effort worthwhile. Don't expect it for every period of extra effort because that's the work you were hired to do. Long periods of extra effort that result in the company making more money or significant advances in your project are the type of situations that are rewarded. If you receive a reward, be it monetary or just a plaque, accept it and sincerely thank the person who nominated you for it and awarded it to you, even if you felt it wasn't enough. Something is always better than nothing.

When money is involved, the greater the achievement, the higher the dollar amount. Occasionally a plaque accompanies the money and sometime the artifact arrives alone. Coincidentally, it often makes an excellent paperweight for all that extra work passing through your hands. After the awards are given out and the patter of congratulatory applause dies off, make it your responsibility to offer all recipients a handshake with sincere and hearty congratulations — regardless of your feelings for them. Why? Because you may be wrong in what you believe about that person.

This is different from being insincere and offering praise or congratulations when it's not worthy because you feel it's the politically correct response. Well, *sometimes* it is the best course of action and you will discover when. The point is that when a peer of yours is awarded for efforts that do not seem outstanding to you, view it without involving yourself. Maybe there was some aspect of his work that you are not aware of, or perhaps he just promoted his work better than you did yours. His project could have higher political clout in the organization than yours. Insincerity is the most easily detectable emotion. Once it is detected in you, you're forever tainted. A close cousin to insincere wishes is blatant flattery, oftentimes directed at a boss, and commonly referred to as ass kissing. No one likes to admit it, but everybody has to do a little. Just don't get windburn from it.

Anger

It's never a good idea to lose your temper with someone at work. I don't care how crazy they may be or how they provoked you, once you raise your voice, the balance of power is transferred to them. Suddenly *you're* the one with the problem. If you absolutely feel that you can't control yourself, go for a walk, find someplace to cool off, or even talk it out with a trusted colleague or anyone who will be objective and respect your confidentiality. It helps if they are familiar with the other person. You don't necessarily need someone to tell you that you're right and he's wrong; you need somebody not too far removed from the environment to talk *at*. In doing so you, as well as the person you're venting to, hear your words. This whole process can be very cathartic. Don't whine, which is cultivating sympathy by complaining and not being receptive to a solution. If you're five years old, that's okay and you can even stamp your feet a little, but not as an adult. The person you speak with may provide you with another perspective on what the other person meant, or just agree with how you're feeling at the moment.

However, if someone has offended you in some manner, and later comes to his/her senses and offers an apology, accept it and let the bad water flow under the bridge.

"Holding on to anger is like grasping a hot coal with the intent of throwing it at someone else; you are the one who gets burned."
— Buddha

Battle stations!

Conflict is a natural occurrence in our lives. If the sparks begin to fly in a public area of work, consider suggesting that you both find an empty conference room to further discuss or argue the issue. Mimic your adversary's posture; stand if he is standing or sit if he is — never choose the opposite. Then listen and gather facts. Getting red-faced and yelling back, challenging or threatening physical confrontation isn't the correct way to handle it. Neither is letting it pass. If you are able or are given the opportunity to respond to your adversary, do so with as much restraint as you are able — don't feed the fire they're breathing. After the confrontation, speak to your manager to keep him informed as to what occurred, and then to your adversary. You can suggest a meeting of all three of you to discuss the issue. If you felt your adversary's attack was both unprofessional and unjustified, now is the time to speak up. If you *were* in the wrong, your adversary should have focused on the problem at hand; belittling you or speaking about you or your work in a degrading manner is not acceptable. I would exercise caution if you feel the need to speak to your adversary alone; involve a third party with some managerial authority. If HR should be called in, so be it, but remember, they're neither your friends nor your enemies; they act in the best interests of the company.

The best approach is to resolve things yourself, which will require you to stand up for yourself against some difficult characters. Again, *listen* to what your opponent is saying. Does he completely understand your point? Do you know what you are talking about? Are you in over your head or out of your area of expertise?

Here's an example of a conflict I had and how I *mismanaged* it: I worked with an arrogant fellow who didn't understand the concept of consideration for other people. One day I was searching in my work area for a vessel of material that I had prepared earlier in the week and now needed to use. I looked on the shelf where I placed it and in adjacent areas, all the while becoming increasingly frustrated. On a hunch, I walked to this fellow's work area, where I promptly found the container of material – *empty!* I was so angry that he used all the material I prepared without asking me and then left the container empty! I went to his office and told him, in no uncertain terms, how inconsiderate I felt he was, how come he can't return things, prepare his own material, and on and on. He was very surprised, to say the least, at how angry I was. He complained to our mutual boss and mentioned that this was the first time he had seen me angry. Mr. Manager sent each of us to people-management courses, instead of getting the two of us together in a conference room to hash out this conflict. The fact that this guy depleted my material wasn't the real source of my anger. *That* incident was the straw that broke the proverbial camel's back. It will have to suffice to say that this fellow had a habit of leaving mutual work spaces a mess and generally being arrogant and ignorant during his interactions with others. *My* mistake was not speaking to him when he laid the *first* straw, and letting it build up so much that his leaving the container empty caused me to get very upset. Also, I did not deliver my tirade correctly. I didn't constrain my words to *what he did* and communicate how it made me feel.

When you're angry at someone, it's difficult not to make your comments personal. A lot of us say "*You* did this. . .", "*You* always. . .", "Why don't *you*. . . ", "Whenever *you*. . ." Using the work "you" puts him, the offender, on the defensive and essentially mutes the other comments. A better way for me to approach the person I mentioned previously would have been to say "I was trying find the bottle of material I prepared yesterday. After twenty minutes I finally located it in our shared work area only to discover the bottle was empty. I don't like having to spend a lot of time looking for things that I prepared in advance for my use and then spend more time preparing them again. This frustrates me because it impedes my productivity. I have no problem sharing, but please let me know when something is removed from my area. Also, after emptying the bottle, the courteous thing to do is to prepare more."

Notice that there isn't a "you" in there. I will be the first to say that speaking like this when you are angry/frustrated/pissed off requires a lot of practice and steel will. In fact, it was difficult for me to *write* that response for you to read. All you may want to do is throttle the person, but you can't, even though that's what some people seem to need in order to get their attention. The point here is *not* to dip your words in chocolate but to minimize accusatory comments. Yes, I know that sounds counter-intuitive, but we're not training wild animals here—people require different treatment. Just be clear and concise about how you feel. Try to do this. I failed in this instance and in others, but in a few occasions I handled it correctly.

Another mistake I made when dealing with the aforementioned person is that I gave him many chances. The initial few instances when he behaved in a similar fashion I overlooked it, chalking it up to his lack of experience and youth, me not wanting to confront him, etc. I naively thought that he would change and people, at least adults, do not—they may mellow (a nice word for hot-tempered people reducing the degree of their anger) but they do not accomplish a complete change in their fundamental behavior. In my opinion, the rate of recidivism, especially for inconsiderate people is one hundred percent. Remember this if you decide to marry.

Get your facts together, double check them, and speak truthfully in a professional manner and keep your temper under control. Be sure of your territory, and don't be blunt; explain carefully what is wrong and what you suggest as a course of action.

My advice is to always tell it the way it is and do it promptly. Hedging, being evasive or vague won't get you anywhere, because many problems don't just go away on their own.

"This guy has no idea what the *(expletive)* he's doing," is best rephrased by saying the person in question "... is possibly mistaken on some fundamental critical issues." Be precise in your viewpoint and make sure that YOU have your facts as straight as an arrow.

Learning to love the know-it-all

The word arrogance is defined in *Webster's Ninth New Collegiate*

Dictionary as "a feeling or an impression of superiority manifested in an overbearing manner or presumptuous claims." Arrogant people have an overbearing, headstrong attitude that their opinions and thoughts are the final word, and everybody else is incorrect and a jackass for thinking differently. *Sometimes they may be correct,* but it's their *delivery* that sends a standoffish "My, aren't you an idiot" vibe. It isn't a quality that is admired.

It's difficult not to admire someone who really knows his/her subject matter and who is also humble. Not self-effacing, just a regular person. It can be an excellent learning opportunity to work with someone like this though if he/she has an arrogant side you will have to deal with that issue. Although it would be nice, there isn't any rule that this type of person is supposed to be a kind, understanding, nurturing pedagogical fellow so you have to tolerate that side of his/her personality.

Circumstances dictated that I work closely with a colleague who was very bright but also known to have an arrogant side. When we began to collaborate, I listened to what he had to say and let the arrogance slip by. I acknowledged his many good ideas, realized the breadth of his expertise and grew to admire him. Over time we became friends. While he didn't exactly reciprocate, he at least became more down to earth with me and easier to deal with. Some respect developed between us.

It can be helpful to cultivate friendships with know-it-alls, but be sure to acknowledge any assistance you receive from them. For example, suppose you're working in tax accounting, where the rules seem to change every year, and you're stuck on some ambiguous situation. The know-it-all in that field can come to your rescue, as can a finite element analysis expert can check your calculations, and the project scheduling wizard can inspect your project plans. It's actually better for *someone* to find an error before it becomes public.

Managing brain flatulence

Consider this scenario: You're in a meeting, discussing a problem, and someone tosses out a suggestion that is absolutely ridiculous. Clearly the person has no idea how ridiculous his idea is, and for some reason, the ball was tossed to you to implement the suggestion. You politely suggest some reasons that this idea isn't feasible, but your words aren't successful in killing the idea. The idea is *still* out there and *you're* asked to produce some data to prove your point. And it's driving you crazy to spend your time making numbers to prove that the concept of this idea is baseless. I've heard this kind of idea referred to as a *brainfart*.

Unfortunately, sometimes you have to produce data to shut people up. You see, unless everyone is on your side and as a group rise up and confirm this person's idiocy, the idea will still be out there. The person with the idea can bring it up again and again, and all you have to go on is your opinion. A former boss of mine used to say, "If you don't have data, you don't have anything." You need some *facts* from a calculation, experiment, test, or some source to put the suggestion to bed once and for all. It won't help you to stew about it. Rant to a trusted colleague to try and make yourself feel better, and then do at least the minimum amount of work required to prove your case. Hope that the next idea of this type doesn't come from a high-level manager who can drag it on and on and on and on. "How about if we changed this, would that make it feasible? Or if we changed that or that or that?" I took out this kind of frustration at the gym I belong to and was eventually able to bench press over 200 lbs.!

If you don't act on the suggestion, you can be in a future meeting on the same topic with the same people and discover that:

- The problem the team is working on is getting worse.
- The team leader asks if there are any stones unturned.

- The owner of the impractical suggestion mentions his or her idea—again.
- The team leader asks who was charged to check this suggestion out.
- The originator of the suggestion mentions that it was delegated to you.
- Everyone in the room turns to look at you for a status update.
- You try to prevent everyone from thinking you're a slacker.
- You are charged with implementing the suggestion immediately.
- The idea turns out to be the key to the team's success and if implemented close to when it was suggested, countless hours of work would have been saved.
- The originator of the then-brilliant idea beams with pride while on your annual performance review there are words indicating you "don't work well with others", or that you're "not a team player."

Here are some things to keep in mind when you have to follow up on a delegated task from the above scenario:

- Make sure that you completely understand the idea. Meet privately with the person who suggested it to comprehend the logic, if there is any.
- Summarize it in a document and send it back to the originator of the idea. Include that you want to be sure you understand the concept before pursuing it further. Consider including the team leader in this note. Perhaps if he sees the idea again, he may suggest abandoning it or think of an easier way of implementing it. Wait for a response before you proceed. For a short while (the time it takes for them to respond) this puts the ball back in his court.
- Assess what you have to do. If the idea is complicated, make

a timeline and project the costs, effort and any additional personnel that may be required. Document any special materials or equipment you require. Start doing the work, but document any roadblocks you encounter or anticipate. You have, during this process, created plenty of feedback for a progress report at the next team meeting. With this approach, the work is getting done and you have covered your behind efficiently.

The interrupter

There are some individuals that I believe are put on this earth to argue. They just *have to* say what's on their mind. A fellow I worked with who was much senior to me had very strong and sometimes controversial opinions. At a meeting, someone would be speaking about an idea, and if he heard something that he felt was incorrect, he would tailgate onto their words with a "No-no-no-no-no-no-no!" and then continue on with his thoughts and corrections. To me, his negation sounded like a difficult-to-start car I once had. In spite of this affectation, I liked and respected this fellow. It might surprise you what you learn to deal with.

You may ask how to deal with a person like this. If he is correct in what he says or offers remarkable insight to the topic, it is best, in my opinion, to accept his manner as a personal quirk and smile inwardly when he goes off.

When an interrupter spouts a comment that, while valuable, could have waited, that is completely incorrect, off topic, or inappropriate, you can say "I'm sorry Edgar. Did the middle of my sentence interrupt the beginning of yours?"

The key here is knowing when to just let it go. Everybody is annoying in their own way.

The art of the schmooze

In an earlier chapter I referred to it as *networking* but a better word is *schmooze*. Don't contrive the image of a slick salesman in a garish plaid suit selling second-rate cars to unsuspecting buyers. Schmoozing is *not* manipulating, though it can help things go in a different direction.

Anytime you interact with a fellow earthling for the purpose of gathering or disseminating information, you are schmoozing. For example, at most professional conferences, a time is set aside for the attendees to drink, eat high-fat appetizers, and tell each other about themselves. This is when you make contacts with vendors and colleagues, and is prime schmooze time. If you're at the gym and you ask the person on the treadmill next to yours who they pick to win the Superbowl, you're schmoozing. When you chat it up with the attractive person next to you in the cafeteria line, you're schmoozing (with dash of flirting on the side). When you schmooze, network, or whatever you wish to call it, you are making yourself known. Schmoozing can help you meet new people and make friends, or even create nucleation sites for future career opportunities. It is important to do it frequently but not just for knowing people who can help you. Your intent should appear to be friendly and forthcoming with other people you encounter.

During a period of this activity, remember that it's listening, not just hearing. People usually like to talk about themselves so you have to be willing to listen *and* pay attention. Don't drift off and if you do, spring back by saying something like "I'm sorry I didn't get that. How did you get that client to offer you a discount?" Of course, "As ye schmooze, so shall ye be schmoozed." They might want to hear about you. So talk. Don't brag, but don't minimize your accomplishments, either. Invariably you'll encounter people who love to hear themselves talk. You'll know them because you won't be saying anything—but you may learn something from them. Sometimes what you learn is how not to be boorish or how to feign an emergency need for the restroom to extricate yourself.

Beyond career leads, the more people you know, the more you can learn—about *life*. New perspectives on topics, from what someone else does for fun to exotic tastes in music—all of this helps make you a well-rounded person. Don't get in the habit of going into a situation just to see how you can benefit. Go in open-minded and act on any opportunity for you to help someone else.

Then there are people who network *constantly*. While they are speaking with you, or listening to you tell a story, they are continually looking around, waving to someone they know who is passing by, looking at that person, checking out that girl's figure, fidgeting, fidgeting, eyes darting left, right, up, down—you want to pepper what you were saying with some outrageous statement just to see if they are paying attention. Everybody does this to some extent, but try to avoid extremes. It can be difficult when someone you need to speak with comes into your field of view. The other extreme, maintaining constant eye contact with someone, can be kind of creepy.

And you are...?

Remembering people's names is generally admired. Addressing a person by his/her name is flattering, and makes it difficult for you to be ignored. The person you address, however, may not remember your name, which may make you feel slighted in some manner. After all, *you* remembered their names, why can't *they* remember *yours?* The reason is that *they* aren't *you*. I've always been pretty good at remembering names. I'll go up to someone I once worked with and say "Sam! Nice to see you! How's Emily? Is Jason still playing lead tuba in the band?" And these people look at me like I have two heads or maybe they feign some recognition, but truth be known, they don't remember who the hell I am. Sometimes, if I want this person to remember me, I'll throw them a hint by incorporating my name into what I'm saying: "My wife said to me the other day, **'Frank,** why don't we..."' Then I watch them light up because NOW they know who I am, even though I had to tell them.

If you are in a conversation with two or more people, use their names if you are referring to one of them. For example, if you and your colleagues Barbara and Phillip are discussing something, don't say, when speaking to Barbara about Phillip "I think **he** might benefit from..." The correct way, that doesn't treat Phillip as if he's invisible, is "I think **Phillip** might benefit from..." A person's name is music to his ears. It conveys that you're recognizing him as an individual, not some disembodied spirit.

The difference between education and intelligence

At some point in your career, you may work with someone who has less education than you. Maybe they have a 2-year degree to your 4-year degree or master's, or they might not have any formal education after high school. The thing to remember about education and intelligence is this: Having one doesn't guarantee having the other. Intelligence is God-given. It's being born with a certain mental horsepower. Education, however, can be acquired through school or through many years on the job or self-study. On-the-job experience can be a very good teacher and might be indistinguishable from purchased, formal education. In combination with high intellect, it's unstoppable. And someone may have spent many years in institutions becoming educated, but have the intelligence of a box of rocks. If you disregard a co worker's advice due a difference in your education, it will be difficult to get his assistance in the future—when you finally realize the value of his knowledge. He may be forced to help you out, but your superior attitude quenched the teamwork spirit. You *have to be sensitive to people's feelings;* mismanaged interpersonal dynamics can be a root cause behind many unfavorable workplace issues. The same advice applies to an older worker. Oliver Wendell Holmes is quoted as saying "The young man knows the rules, but the old man knows the exceptions." Experience is a very good teacher, and the experienced person has played the course you are on before—many times. I could not locate the origin of this quote, but you should commit it to memory: "Old age and treachery will always overcome youth and skill." The wisdom of old(er) age is multi-faceted. Be careful who you dismiss as "expired."

So a key component of succeeding is being able to get along with people. I'm not saying that you have to be a warm-and-fuzzy teddy bear, never crossing anyone lest you make them frown. *That is* a recipe for disaster, because people will eat you alive. Just try and be, for lack of a better word, *common*. Also, understand the difference between hearing and listening to people. Many people hear others ideas but do not *listen* to them. A natural tendency when someone is speaking to you is to plan your response to them. *Hearing* is the process when your auditory organs receive sound, relay it to your brain, which interprets it as speech. *Listening* is doing all that, but with the extra effort to understand the reasoning behind the other person's thoughts. Don't be the person who doesn't understand where someone's thoughts or misunderstanding are coming from.

- People can easily sense insincerity, and it is a label that's difficult to remove.
- Admit when you're wrong.
- Don't be the first to point out someone else's mistake but if you must, don't make it a big deal.
- If you need to borrow something, ask the owner first. If it's an emergency and you can't find them to ask, leave a note stating such and return the item promptly.
- Clean up any mess you make in your work area.
- Treat everyone the same—with respect.

This includes everyone from the corpulent VP to the janitor who empties your wastebasket, especially the janitor who empties your wastebasket. When he comes your area to mop or collect the trash, thank him. While no one may thank you for doing your job, these people are generally treated as invisible and are taken for granted. Remember, you are no better than anyone else.

"This is the final test of a gentleman:
His respect for those who can be of no possible service to him."
— William Lyon

Never dismiss any task by saying that you will just . . . give it to the (tech, clerk, contract, or other subordinate) to do." Always request the contribution that anyone could make to the project by saying that "Perhaps Rudolph would be able to help us by ordering the supplies we need." Or ask the person directly "Would you help us with this?" It's always a team effort. Your support personnel can make or break you. Be easy to work with: state your expectations clearly, be available for questions, and publicly acknowledge everyone's contribution. And be willing to change your course of action and acknowledge when someone finds an error in your proposed method.

Chapter 10
Getting Ahead

"The man on top of the mountain did not fall there."
—from a fortune cookie I opened

Wisdom and insight can be found in so many places and from many different people. The day I took my mother to lunch at the Royal Dynasty in Webster, NY, our favorite Chinese restaurant, the message in my fortune cookie was particularly significant. The fortune is a distillation of the secret to success, which, before someone coerces you to pay them to tell you, I will provide for free: *there is no secret—it's all hard work.* Sure, you can marry someone who has a lot of money or whose family has a successful business, but most people go it alone and work their way to the top.

"The only place success comes before work is in the dictionary."
– Vince Lombardi

Some people might feel that I shouldn't be giving advice on how to advance in a company since I never advanced to a managerial position. I maintained a level of sustained above-average performance, many times excelling and a few times my yearly performance was described as *outstanding*. But when it came to promotions, I realized after about fifteen years into my career that if I stayed at the company where I was, I probably wouldn't be promoted. I did not like the responsibilities given to a person at grade levels higher than mine. I liked the idea of being promoted, especially the increased salary, and my bosses gave me the opportunity to show them I had what it takes. For many reasons, I felt that what it took was not something I enjoyed.

There weren't any terrible technical or intellectual challenges in the "promotable" activities. I'm a hands-on technical person and dislike discussing the schedule for deliverables, discussing project plans, project goals, project timelines, problems interfering with the aforementioned goals, plans, and timelines, how to manage those problems, who was responsible for the problems, what was the timeline for solving the problems, what were the short and long term impact of those problems on our goals and timelines, should we change our goals and timelines, if so, how much, where there any work-arounds to the problems, could the problems be categorized as critical, major, or ordinary. This entailed having a big-picture view of the project and quite honestly, I did not want to or like thinking at that level. I realized I might be at a crossroads in my career, and had the feeling that I had more satisfying and meaningful goals than dealing with those seemingly inane concerns. What were those more satisfying and meaningful goals? At the time, I did not have a clue. Today, my answer to you is what you're reading is one of them. So I realized that I could be a valuable and productive contributor to the company, not have to do the big-picture stuff, not feel pressured to do something that felt unnatural, and figure out where I was going with my life. Truthfully, I don't have any bitterness about not being promoted. It took a while for me to realize that if I wanted to stay with the company that employed me, it was just fine for me to be me. It would have saved me some angst if one of my bosses along the way had spoken candidly with me about my aspirations and what would have been expected from me.

With all that I've told you about my career, remember that my experience is far from the only way it has to be. There are plenty of people where I worked who had my love of the laboratory and also excelled at the project manager stuff. And there are some who should have never set foot in a lab. This is my experience—your opportunity, because you are an individual, different from anyone else in the world, and at an altogether different company, won't necessarily resonate with my experience.

I have, however, thoroughly observed many people at various levels of management, seen who gets promoted for what kinds of activities, and noted how they worked,—*that* is why I can write about advancement. I was in the war but didn't get any medals.

Let's continue.

Even though you may be a law-abiding, well-educated person, when you accept a job at a company, you require a foundation to build on. And while the analogy to a flower nurtured in fertile soil might be trite, it's accurate. For you, the fertilizer for the soil is your reputation. Sometimes it's referred to as work ethic, attitude, persona or even curb appeal. Call it what you like, but it's your most important quality.

As a new employee you typically don't start at or near the top of any organization's food chain. There is a *learning curve* for you to traverse. The world of work requires that you first prove yourself competent in tasks that may not appear that important or challenging, perhaps on a less exciting task that everyone else has been successful in avoiding.

Your boss and colleagues will be forming opinions of you and deciding if you can be trusted on more complicated and interesting problems, on the basis of how well you accomplish the initial duties they feed you.

If you work extremely diligently when you start a new job, people notice and their perception of you becomes increasingly favorable. It rises from neutral. Their perception colors your boss's perception and so on up the line. Get enough positive perception and credibility is established, which means that people can trust the output you produce. Perception goes beyond the surface. Those who think, foolishly, that they have only to *look* diligent are in for a rude awakening as no one can fool everyone. And once someone sees that you are a slacker, it fuels a wildfire.

It's extremely difficult to ascend from a negative initial reputation to a positive one. People always recall their first impression of you. Come across as lazy, ignorant, unwilling to learn and difficult to work with, and you might have to perform miracles to make people think differently. A positive initial impression, however, takes some work to destroy. But it can be done.

"You can't build a reputation on what you're going to do."
— Henry Ford

How are positive impressions generated?

- Arrive a little earlier and stay a little later than the people around you, even 15 minutes. But don't spend the extra time drinking coffee or reading the newspaper. Don't have a spring in your chair at five o'clock. Deliver more than what is expected of you. A former boss of mine would advise "under-commit and over-deliver."

- Ask questions and pay attention to what everyone else is saying. Become attuned to how the people in your department think and talk to each other. How do they approach problems? If you have an idea for a possible solution to a problem that they have been working on, don't discount it as probably worthless. By all means, think your idea through and test the waters by discussing it with your boss.

- Don't approach your boss with problems until you are able to state calmly and clearly exactly what the problem is and – this is important – what are your ideas on how to solve it.

- Never present a problem to your boss with a table of numbers. Instead, show him a graphical presentation so he will quickly understand what you are saying. The first thing he would do with a table of numbers is to create a graph and then study it and while he may come to the same conclusion as you, he had to do more work to get to that point. Study it before you present it and ask yourself "What are these data telling me?" Convey your thoughts to your boss about the message within the data. You don't have to recommend the solution, just make an honest attempt to show that you're not afraid to think. If you have an idea for a solution, present it to your boss and ask for his feedback. Remember, you're learning and this is why I've said to enjoy the learning curve. You also are trying to demonstrate that you can think.

- Function in as many respects as possible like a person at the next higher grade in your organization
- Through your accomplishments, convince as many people as possible at the next higher grade level and in management that you are already working at that level, and recommend that you be promoted.

Observe those at the next level up from you in your organization, and try to understand what type of decisions they have to make and how they think. Attend their presentations, since these will be representative of the work they are doing and the problems, issues, etc. that they deal with. Listen to what they say and how they speak in meetings. What kind of questions do they ask in those high-level communication meetings? Can they make sense of what the VP is saying?

I rarely understood high-level presentations; 10 minutes into them and I was in la-la land. I would go to the meetings and say to myself *"This time* I'm going to get something out of this." I would bring a pad and pen to take notes. The speaker would begin and my attention span was like an airplane banking into a turn. It was always a bunch of slides with fine print and a lot of arrows, never plain English. I understood the individual words they said, but when they combined them into a sentence, it was gibberish to me.

Successful managers have the ability to look at the big picture and understand it from both a business and technical point— how will it make money for, or fit into the goals of the company and what technical aspects drive it. Having the ability to see the big picture is extremely valuable, as it conveys that you know how your job, your department's goals, and goals of departments adjacent to yours integrate into the corporation.

Seeing the big picture can be challenging, so take smaller steps initially. Focus on how your job and those of your colleagues fit into your own department. Then expand to include adjacent departments, etc., and don't be afraid to ask your boss for explanations.

During your annual performance appraisal, you can initiate a discussion if you are functioning in line with promotional guidelines. The buzz-words that will be mentioned are:

- Sustained performance (are you performing at a consistent level or getting better at what you do?),
- Time in grade (how long have you been doing what you do?),
- Skill business value (does the company or its competitors need what you do?),
- Peer performance (is there anyone in your type of job performing better than you?)
- Management evaluation (what do your boss and the other bosses think of you?).

A main obstacle to getting a promotion is convincing the committee to grant you one. It is not unlike becoming a "made" man in an organized crime syndicate. A key component is *having someone, usually a senior member of the organization, in your corner who sings your praises and vouches for your promotion*. One method of finding that person is by having a *mentor*. In the ideal case, they know your capabilities and shortcomings as well as you, perhaps even better than you. It is even more helpful if they're well thought of and higher up in the organization.

The medical field is rife with mentoring relationships. They refer to them as *residencies*. A physician friend of mine described them as a situation where "you are someone's 'bitch' for three or four or five or six years." In industry, a direct mentoring relationship, where your mentor is your immediate supervisor, can be advantageous. Your mentor-boss will eventually send you to meetings in his stead, and allow you to present data, plans, etc. You build or augment your reputation with technical competence and expertise.

---

*A mentor can give you the opportunity to think and speak
on your own with some guidance on the side. They are
not grandparent-like men and women with a warm, fuzzy,
understanding and nurturing manner.*

They can be described as taskmasters or even *tormentors* because they'll expect a lot from you. That's the way you learn—by doing. It doesn't have a formal indoctrination ceremony and in fact, it's better if you pick your mentor. As you begin your job and learn who does what for whom, you'll find people who you are drawn to, perhaps in admiration for their expertise or influence. Maybe it will be your boss or someone you work with. It's hard to describe accurately since it's an evolving situation. In your dealings with this individual, you can get a feel for how he/she works and if possible, begin to form some sort of friendship based on mutual respect: you respect this person's experience, knowledge, and character and he/she respects you for being someone willing to work hard, learn, and help in what he/she is trying to achieve. This person can be someone who sees that you get opportunities. And you're not using him or her.

You don't get down on one knee and ask someone to be your mentor, but you can express your acknowledgment of their skills and expertise and mention how you would like to work with—and learn—from them. Your company may in fact have a formal mentoring or development program for new hires.

Three additional factors affecting a promotion are your visibility, achievements, and communication:

• Being known. People, especially your superiors, have to know you beyond as a name on an organization chart. They need to know what things you've done for the company and how well you did them.

- Being seen. Specifically, your contribution to the company should be seen along with your face and name so that a link is created. Attend presentations by senior management (and stay awake and alert), and other company functions like holiday parties. This is called getting *face time*.

- Being heard. Increase your visibility and illustrate your achievements by presenting your work at meetings, seminars, workshops, project reviews, and other places where your peers and superiors gather. Presenting material is an excellent way to demonstrate your competence. I'll be discussing presentations in more detail in a later chapter.

Being solid

Your attitude toward your job is apparent to your colleagues and superiors. It's not something that can be disguised to fool everyone. Other qualities to have are a good work ethic, and competence in your field of endeavor. Each of these aspects alone doesn't do much for you except make people notice which of the other two are missing. The truly solid people I've known had good attitudes, were easy to speak with, and facilitated the work process. They were honest about what they could do, were clear about what they were asking of others, listened attentively to what other people had to say, had a sense of humor, didn't have any hidden agendas, and treated everyone with respect. These are truly rock *solid* people. My father was rock *solid, as* were many of my former professors. Several of my bosses were solid characters as well as many of my colleagues. I've known many other solid people and I'm sure you will also. Remember who they are and how they act; when you're stuck on an issue, it can be helpful to think what they would do.

In many companies, a non-effective, "slippery" person is tolerated, because people, including high level managers can be fooled by sexy presentations with corporate buzz-speak and fuzzy, minuscule graphs and diagrams of incomplete data that are merely props for their show. It may seem to be mostly "smoke and mirrors." There are others who are certainly employed, but no one knows exactly *what* they do. Somehow, when there's a crisis they aren't around. They start things going, then when the work has to be done, they suddenly have a meeting several buildings away.

Consistently leaving your workplace early can influence someone's impression of you. We all have appointments with the dentist, doctor, traffic court or whatever. And employers generally understand that. If you are always on the "taking" side, it will catch up with you and could make its way to your performance appraisal where it is documented permanently. If it's the *first* time it has been put in writing, it means that someone, perhaps in a position of authority, noticed it enough times that it needed to be documented. Make sure that it is never mentioned again.

The way to manage this is to be "square" about your time. If you have to cut out an hour early, on another day stay an hour or more later to make up for it; consider sending a brief note to your boss to tell him what you're doing. You don't necessarily have to tell him the gory details, just that you have some personal business or if it's the truth, a medical or dental appointment. It's true that as a professional you don't have to punch a clock, but the work still has to get done. You can't say that you'll just work harder and accomplish what you're supposed to because that begs the question as to why aren't you always working at that pace? A salaried person is still as responsible for putting in a 40-hour week as an hourly person is. The difference is the absence of a time clock and the higher wage for the salaried person because they are expected to go above and beyond on a regular basis. The hourly person gets overtime when necessitated and has to account for his time, but the salaried people, because they are routinely arriving early and leaving later can move about with less rigor. They are expected to put in casual overtime which means that they are not reimbursed for it.

Consider this scenario: For some reason you desire to *regularly* leave your job at Fabulous Flanges at 4:00 instead of the 5:00 norm for your organization. Being the diligent person you are, you arrive promptly at work at 7:00 am and when the situation requires, even earlier. With the usual unpaid hour for lunch, you are putting in an honest day's work. But you pass Mr. Manager's office on your way out the building and all this guy sees is you always leaving at 4:00 pm. He *doesn't* know that you were already hard at work while he was on the toilet reading the morning paper and that you are not cheating the company out of an hour. While he is incorrect if he thinks you have been cheating the company an hour, everybody else is working till 5:00. What happens if someone needs your expertise at 4:30? "Tough tamales" isn't the right answer. The *company* is structured around 8 to 5 but *you* have to leave at 4:00. If it's the exception rather than the rule, there will probably not be a problem. Everyone understands that there are appointments that cannot be scheduled after 5pm. When husband and wife both work, and one of the children becomes ill, usually one of the parents has to leave. These are very understandable and reasonable instances for leaving work early. But with exercise classes, entertainment plans, and similar activities, you should schedule your life around the company, which is paying you to be there and work with everyone else. Now if your company allows flex time, where you schedule your time as I've described earlier, all I can say is to use your best judgment. Sometimes, appearance counts more than you think.

Another fact: leaving five minutes early every day for a typical year of two hundred thirty eight working days, give or take, amounts to 1190 minutes, or *almost three days!* Try asking your boss if he minds if you take an extra three days of paid vacation. "Only five minutes" is understandable but not on a regular basis. Treat your time like a savings account: put some in so that you have something to take out later.

In most corporations, employees are given paid time off when they are unable to come to work due to illness or injury. Some employers allocate a chunk of time to be used as paid time off for whatever the reason – illness, injury, vacation, jail time – everything is lumped together and once it's gone, it's gone. On a dreary, rainy Monday, though, you'll be tempted to deal out one of those precious sick days and claim to be "very sick and unable to make it in today", spoken with a gravelly voice to sound convincing, maybe spicing it up by mentioning countless hours of involuntary bodily functions. And maybe after consuming some odd tasting chicken wings at the Superbowl party the previous evening it *will* be true. Or maybe the *thought* of coming into work is making you ill. One reason I speak out against playing hooky is because it can affect your credibility. After all, it isn't the truth. Saying to yourself that you were sick— sick of work, that is—is a poor rationalization. Justifying your laziness with stories of CEOs stealing from their employees' pension accounts just doesn't cut it. It moves you a notch closer to them. If you need time off, burn one of your vacation days. Some companies allow their employees to buy an extra week's vacation by deducting the cost from their salary *over the entire year.* That takes some of the sting out. Save the sick time for when you're truly ill, whether it is the flu or extended dental work.

If your partner or parent or other loved one is seriously ill and you need to be at the hospital or attend to them, make sure you inform your boss. Let them know what is going on and that you may require a more flexible schedule for some period of time. Deadlines may not change, but perhaps some of your responsibilities can be distributed to your colleagues. Continue to at least make the effort to do what's expected of you and keep your boss informed if some task is going to be late. Communication is the key.

The companies where I've worked have been very family friendly, but if your boss or company is going to be a bastard about taking time off from work, you have to make the choice. While I don't know your situation, I do know that for me, my job comes first—right after my family and personal health, never before.

A manager of mine once told me that in order to advance "you have to learn to make decisions based on limited information." At first I didn't understand what he meant. He didn't mean to skip every fourth data point or do a partial experiment and predict the outcome. What he was referring to is the self-confidence to make decisions using your own judgment. I would frequently discuss things with my bosses because I thought it was important that they be kept in the loop—which they did want—but maybe I didn't develop or convey a sense of independent thought on my part. I was considered an above-average or even outstanding performer, but that alone doesn't necessarily lead to advancement.

It's easy to pass everything through the boss—a problem, decisions, quantity of supplies to order, whatever—and in some cases he may be a micro-manager and want—or even *demand*—that it be that way. Another approach is to start small and start making some decisions on your own, or at least have some idea or thought or concept in your mind *before* you speak with your boss. Take five minutes, sit down at your desk, and think the problem through before you go talk to him. Rather than state the situation and look helpless, *explain* the situation and then explain what you think is the right action to take. At the very least, offer him your thoughts on what happened, and what you are thinking of doing to rectify the situation. When you have a problem, don't panic. Take a deep breath, step back from the problem, and begin to brainstorm approaches to its solution. We would hope, though, you're not operating a nuclear reactor or guiding a ship around some icebergs.

"It's not that I'm so smart, it's just that I stay with problems longer."
— Albert Einstein

Dr. Einstein had a unique way of looking at things *and a* superior intellect, but the point is that staying with a problem — persistence — is a key attribute. The trick is to know when you have arrived at the point of diminishing returns, when you're just spinning your wheels and can't conceive of a solution. You also have to realize when there is a true emergency and you shouldn't spend additional time analyzing problem. That's the time to ask for assistance. If there's a manufacturing line that is stalled while you solve a problem, it doesn't matter if you get the solution from a Ouija board as long as it gets things moving.

Chapter 11
Dealing with Discontentment and Disillusionment

"When you come to a fork in the road, take it." — Yogi Berra

"Take this job and shove it—I ain't working here no more"
— Lyrics by David Allan Coe, popularized by Johnny Paycheck

©2010 King Features Syndicate, Inc. World Rights Reserved.

I understand how easy it is easy to become disillusioned. During the interview, you were being courted and everyone was on their best behavior; everything looked fresh and exciting and the world was full of new experiences and possibilities. Now, after several months, you know your way around the building, and things may seem more commonplace. Perhaps you've seen a different side of your boss and new colleagues. Maybe their "Be encouraging and nice to the new hire" attitude has given way to "Do I have to show him *everything?*" The pressures of work can bring out a less-than-attractive side of anyone.

Whatever the reason(s) for the way you feel, make the commitment to stay where you are for at least one year, during which you will be gaining experience in the simple process of working, which encompasses everything from learning and becoming proficient at your job, to putting up with crap from others and knowing when to give it back.

Be patient with yourself. Feelings can change over time—you may begin to love what you hated and hate what you once enjoyed. Give yourself some wiggle room. While it is fair to say that most people have, at least one time in their lives, aspired to say the words in the song by Johnny Paycheck, don't do that. That is called "burning a bridge," meaning that you've established an unfavorable reference which can haunt you when you are asked to provide a detailed work history for future career changes. Press on. Continue to do the best you can, because all jobs have unsatisfying periods. Feelings ebb and flow. And although no one likes to hear "do as I say, not as I do," *don't do what I did* when I quit my first job out of school after six months. Quitting after a short time can be problematic, if, for example, you've signed a year's lease on an apartment or have a monthly car loan for the next several years. No job usually equates to no money, and financial responsibilities without money equals big problems. I was living at home with my parents, who were not thrilled with their son quitting his job. There were plenty of heated discussions, to say the least, following my resignation.

It is fair to say that when their alarm clock rings, very, very few people jump out of bed and say "Yippee! Off to work I go!" Most people get up, somewhat grudgingly, and begin their morning routine. But if day after day and week after week, your first words when the alarm clock goes off are an expletive and "Oh no! Another day!" it's time to do some very serious thinking. Doing this serious thinking isn't easy and I speak from experience.

Quiet contemplation works for some people, but conversing with someone you trust can be helpful. I'm not referring to a bitch session, and although those can be therapeutic, what might be more helpful is a meeting with you and a coach, close friend, parent, sibling, or uncle where you talk about what's going on in your life. You have to ask and begin to answer a few seemingly simple questions:

- "What *exactly* am I unhappy about?" This could be the specific job you're doing, its location, your commute to work, your coworkers, your boss, or what he expects from you, the work load (or lack thereof), where your desk is, and so on. You need to get at the root cause. Is it your job or something else, like feeling lonely or homesick, that is upsetting you?

- "What can I do to improve this situation?" Sometimes a simple thing like getting a better chair or changing where you sit can help matters, but don't ask for a corner office with a window and a door. Perhaps you need to clarify what your boss expects from you or, when it's possible, move closer to work or even a different part of town where there are more activities and people your age.

Making mid-course corrections

You will probably have a performance review after a year which we'd hope would be positive. A favorable performance review is essential if you decide to seek other employment which can be a different department in the same company.

Your performance review is the time to clear up questions you have about your job. If you have some words on your review that mention areas you want to improve on, make sure you understand what is expected of you. Suggesting that you meet regularly to discuss briefly how you are performing in those areas allows you to get mid-course corrections that can help to ensure you're on the right track.

If you have an idea for an improvement or change in a work process, consider discussing it with your boss at your review. By the way, if your boss is quick to dismiss suggestions or resist change, consider prefacing your idea with "It would be a lot easier for me if", "Do you think it's possible to" or "Would it be wrong to suggest". Remember, you are relatively new to this job, so you want to be perceived as someone eager to contribute but not a person who wants to arrive and change everything.

It's okay to zig and zag

Our lives do not always progress in a linear fashion, so don't feel that wanting to leave a company or pursue an entirely different path is something to avoid at all costs. If you ask people about their lives and careers, some might have had many directional changes while others stayed in one place for their entire working lives. I think the important task is to get out there into the workforce *first,* learn what the working world is all about, discover what you like and don't like to do. From my first job I learned that I didn't want to work in routine environments like quality control. Some people just love tracking results, observing trends, developing methods of analysis, doing all kinds of statistical quality control. I just never cared for that. I recognize that it's an important, essential function but it's not one that piques my interest. Every experience you have is grist for the mill, which means that your life is a combination of experiences, chances taken, mistakes made, and fortuitous events, or luck. Put all these together and you grind out a career, not too different from making sausage.

Preparing to make a change

A job with greater satisfaction to you can be in a different department or division of the same company that currently employs you. Most companies have some type of career or job-posting system for open or unfilled positions. One advantage to not changing companies is that you continue to build your time of service and work history at a company. You don't want to get in the habit of jumping ship too quickly, lest your experience becomes one with many short-term jobs. If you were a contract employee, that's a different situation that should be made clear on your resume. If your company contributed to a pension account for you, leaving before you are vested in the plan can prevent you from withdrawing those funds.

Before you discuss a transfer to a different department with your boss, make sure you know what your contributions have been. You need to document concisely what you've been doing, where you've been doing it, and most importantly, what value you brought to your job. Simply put, you have to answer the question "So what?" when you talk about your experience. Did you improve anything or process a record number of claims, collect on a large number of delinquent accounts, attain expertise on a type of software and then teach it to others? Perhaps you presented some problem-solving techniques to a workgroup adjacent to yours. Think long and hard about anything you've done within and outside of your expected responsibilities. These accomplishments in combination with what you were responsible for have the potential to distinguish you from other people and help you understand and present your value to your current and future bosses.

Get clear in your mind what you're looking for in next job you get.

Many people put their resumes aside once they land jobs and resurrect them when they start to feel frustrated or hear rumblings of a downsizing. Don't fall into that trap. A current resume allows you to be one of the first to apply for newly-announced positions or opportunities.

If you don't know what you want, no one else will either, and your uncertainty will be obvious to those who interview you. You can say that you're seeking a position with more growth, but make sure you know what kind of growth you want. Is it project manager within three years followed by group manager within ten more years? Perhaps you don't necessarily want growth, but a greater variety in the things you can do. Or maybe you just want experience in a company that is more financially stable. Or a job that requires less travel. Or more travel. Or allocates more money to research. Or a company that encourages its employees to further their education. You don't want to say that you just want to get away from your psycho boss. Honesty is the best policy and there are better ways to say that. For example, when I've been asked why I was looking for a new position, I said that I'm interested in broadening my experience within the company. That's a nice way of saying "I'm sick of what I'm doing and where I'm working and want to learn something else, somewhere else."

Though it can be challenging to keep your resume in tip-top ready-to-interview shape, you can have a notebook, preferably permanently bound, where you keep track of new responsibilities you've assumed, changes in your project, or at least a big-picture view of what you've been doing every day. Each morning, write down the date, and document that day's activities. Take it to meetings and write your notes from the meetings in it. Note any action items (especially yours) that were assigned in the meeting. Don't worry about the form, punctuation or how you say it, just get the facts down. Sketches, ideas, questions, who said what to whom, and any thoughts you have are all valuable things to record. Remember, it's your notebook. When you have to write a progress report, it will be helpful, providing you were faithful in maintaining it. It takes some discipline to do this and if you become proficient, you'll be the person everyone turns to when there's a question. Everyone notices the person who makes notes in a meeting instead of staring into space.

Of particular value when you are dissatisfied with your job

are the techniques of schmoozing which I introduced earlier. For example, if or when you join your co-workers for lunch or socializing after work, you may meet someone who knows someone at a different company that is looking for an individual with your particular expertise. Or the person you share the office with tells you about an article he read in a trade magazine about a company that you just might kill to work at. You can never predict when a connection will occur.

"Chance favors the prepared mind" is a quote attributed to Louis Pasteur. My interpretation of that is being aware of what you are looking for makes you more apt to recognize an opportunity, unusual result, or something different. I've seen this called heightened awareness.

Being your own boss

Some people are drawn to the idea of entrepreneurship, and others, like myself, realize that they don't have the fortitude for anything of the sort. While you shouldn't just dream about it or tell yourself that it is a stupid idea, you should not resign quickly to pursue it. Realize that it is not for the faint of heart! Be prepared to work like a dog day and night.

I worked with a fellow who decided to start a business doing videos of weddings and the like. He quit his full-time, well-paying job to do the video thing full time. And he didn't even have the business off the ground! We all said he was nuts, because this type of idea is something you start doing after 5 o'clock and on weekends. You acquire the clients, get experience (read as money, excellent feedback from clients, and the benefit of making some mistakes and learning the tricks of the trade) and nurture the business. See where and how it grows, and then, if you see positive trends, make your move. If it doesn't work as a full-time venture you can always do it part time.

I know another fellow who is a "textbook" entrepreneur. He built a product of his own design and he did it full time. He put every cent of his into this venture but there is another wage earner in his life to put food on the table and pay the mortgage. If you and your partner can do this, then go for it, and good luck. But do your research first, and don't expect it to be easy or without setbacks. There are short quizzes around that can help you decide if you have the entrepreneurial spirit. Answer them truthfully, and seek out and talk to entrepreneurs about their experiences. I'm willing to bet that none of them say it was easy. And I think it is important to realize that you have to have considerable fortitude, iron will, confidence, good sense, and the ability to work day and night. If you're not a risk taker, think twice before venturing out on your own.

Another friend of mine who I've known since we were children is a successful musician. The name of the game for him is hustle. He plays in several groups, teaches music privately and in a school, plays music for commercials, composes his own work, and is generally busy all the time. And he loves it.

Yet another friend of mine owns his own business as a distributor for industrial supplies and custom fabricator of mechanical assemblies. He has about twenty people in his company. Fortunately for him, he is very busy, mostly due to his indefatigable work ethic. If he is not out on the road selling, he's attending a trade show or in the office. His travel schedule is a whirlwind tour of the United States; I've seen him at the gym in the evening after a day of driving hundreds of miles to see a customer and then driving the same distance back home. It's constant, but as he says, the buck stops with him. He is responsible for the financial well-being of his employees and himself. Why does he do it? Although I haven't asked him directly, it is probably like this: He's established and successful and obviously needs the money as we all do. Work can be like mind over matter, to paraphrase Mark Twain: If you don't mind, it doesn't matter. If you like it (or don't mind it), it's not really work. It probably satisfies some deeper needs he has, like being his own boss and having more control over what happens in his life.

When you're being shown the door

There are many words for it: downsizing, rightsizing, restructuring, and so on. No matter what it's called, you are unemployed. It happens all the time in all economic conditions. It happened to me. Early one morning, my boss's boss came to my office door. We knew that something was going to happen, so when I heard a knock and saw who it was, my heart was pounding. I said "Hi." She replied "Frank, we have to talk…" For a minute I thought of old girlfriends that began a breakup speech with those same words.

The point here is not to share the gory details and general unpleasant times that followed. My take away message for you, if you are separated from your job, is that it is not the end of the world.

©2009 King Features Syndicate, Inc. World Rights Reserved.

If you are separated from your company, here are some general guidelines to consider:

- Remain calm. Or be as calm as you can be. Getting angry, threatening to pursue legal action, or being excessively tearful will not improve the situation. Maintain your dignity and listen carefully.

- Inquire why you were selected for dismissal. Clarify whether it is for your performance, behavior, some other incident, or as a result of poor financial performance of the company. If they mention any reason other than financial, demand exact details including the names of all personnel involved in the decision.

- Ask whether they will request you be denied unemployment benefits from your state government. Both you and your company have paid into these benefits but if, for example, you were fired because of theft or consistent, inexcusable absenteeism, the company will inform the state of your history which will disallow you from receiving benefits. Your state unemployment benefits are contingent upon you keeping an active job search; you will be expected to provide them the details, such as the names or companies and what position you applied for. While some of the personnel at the state agency may appear to be perfunctory, use every resource available to your advantage.

- Companies are not required to, but frequently give money, called severance or continuance, to employees who are dismissed. You should ask about or request this.

- Outplacement counseling is frequently offered to downsized people. The services offered can vary, but generally consist of meeting with someone from an agency who will coach you on your search for a new job. They may have an office in a local building where you will be allowed to work at your job search, and collaborate with others who are in the same situation you are. There might also be a copier you can use at minimal or no cost. You should register and participate with the agency as long as it is provided to you at no additional cost. I would not pay for any services of this sort: recruiters (employment agencies) will be happy to meet with you and take you on as a client. Confirm with them that they will be paid by the company that hires you and that you, as their client, are not required to pay for any of their services.

- Try and maintain a positive outlook. This is much easier said than done. Your family and friends will undoubtedly offer all kinds of advice, but don't immediately dismiss it. Think about what they have said. Perhaps it can trigger thoughts that may be applicable to your situation.

Chapter 12
The Money

There is a simple message here: Don't fall into the credit card trap!

Getting paid for the first time is always a watershed event. After you get over the amount the government has helped themselves to, but *before* you spend what's left, read some of my guidelines for common sense and rational behavior.

I've witnessed from the sidelines some ugly situations caused by poor money management. You have to differentiate between your *wants* and your *needs*. You *need* a place to live but you may *want* a luxury apartment with wonderful amenities. You *need* a television but you may *want* a costly cable subscription with a thousand channels. You *need* a vehicle but you may *want* an expensive sports car with sizable monthly payments. You can't always have it both ways, unless you 1) have the money in the first place, 2) find someone else to pay your bills, or 3) fall into the trap of credit card debt which is a rampant disease in the United States. I am always astounded when I hear about people with $20,000, $30,000, $40,000 and more on their credit cards. And they pay the minimum every month and are charged loan-shark-level interest rates. It's fair to say that they will be paying off their balances for many, many, many years to come, and with all the interest paid, their purchases will have cost them much more than they realize! If you know someone with significant credit card debt, learn from his or her bad example.

Keep yourself out of additional debt. Don't think you'll be able to put your creditors off—collection agencies have heard every excuse there is, and it's a sure bet you won't be able to give them one they haven't heard a thousand times before. Keep them off your back; you don't need the aggravation.

My recommendation is to start a budget.
Consider every purchase carefully.

Maintain responsible financial behavior

Know your financial obligations, pay those first, and enjoy your life. I'm not telling you to dumpster dive for free food.

You may be responsible for enormous student loans that rival a home mortgage! I feel sorry for you having such a financial burden, but I also admire you for taking charge of your life.

Credit card companies can entice you with reasonable-appearing credit limits and interest rates, but because they're so easy to whip out of your wallet, you can quickly develop considerable *convenience debt*. Consider forgoing a credit card if it will help you follow your budget. Keep the lines of communication open between you and your student loan creditor, and always be prepared to pay *something*. If they want a monthly payment that would force you to live in a cardboard box, you have to renegotiate the terms of your loan and not be bullied by them. Reiterate that you are aware of your obligations and have every intention of meeting them. If you're seeing yourself here, and feel that you are being bullied or harassed, seek out legal aid—*free* legal aid that is. *Pro bono* is another term lawyers use for free.

- Include yourself among your creditors and pay yourself after you take care of the rent, utilities, etc. You pay yourself by regularly saving some of your earnings. The easiest way is to have it deducted from your wages and deposited directly into a savings account.
- If you have a 401k savings plan where your company matches what you contribute up to a certain amount, it's to your advantage to contribute enough to get the maximum that your company pitches in.
- If you can't contribute the maximum without strapping yourself, or if your company doesn't have matched savings, save something every pay period. $25 is something. Even $10. Just get in the habit of saving regularly early in your career.

The cost of accumulative spending

Money, while not being a panacea for job satisfaction, is a fundamental reason that people go to work every day. The amazing thing about money is how fast it can disappear! This is why you should be aware of your spending habits. You should know, to the nearest ten dollars or so, where you spend your money.

Charitable organizations frequently say that supporting them requires only a minimal amount, sometimes pennies, per day. Any charity requires money to do the good things they do, and in order to generate support, they have to convey that small amounts of money given monthly are fairly easy to accommodate in a budget.

But think about how much a few daily expenses can cost over the course of a year:

- $4 daily coffee: $1000
- $12 for lunch at the company cafeteria: $3000
- $50 for weekend socializing: $2400
- $3 at the vending machine: $750

So far, the total is, conservatively, over seven thousand dollars. Pay attention to what you spend. If you are consistently short on cash each month you should know why. Brewing coffee at home and bringing a thermos to work, or brown-bagging it for lunch a few days a week isn't beneath you.

As I write this, Social Security is said to be on shaky grounds; who knows if you can depend on it. You can, however, depend on yourself to create a stable financial future. *Be especially wary about investing your money in stock of the company that employs you.* Your company may offer you attractive opportunities to purchase stock though their 401k plan or by taking bonus dollars as company stock. You are *already* investing in the company as a career so distribute the risk. Invest your money outside of where you are employed because you stand to lose it all should the company traverse troubled times.

Search on the companies *Enron* and *WorldCom* to learn about corruption. People at these companies, some of whom were on the horizon of retirement, lost most of their savings due to crooked management. The head honchos at these companies *lied*. Thankfully, those responsible are in federal prison, but their employees are still out their money.

Absorb information about financial matters

Pay attention during financial discussions. Ask questions. Read the financial page of your local newspaper, listen to podcasts and network broadcasts on the economy. The point is to become mindful of the financial world, and regarding investments, trust no one. Wait, that's not nice. Be *very selective* who you trust.

While I can't attest to the accuracy of their knowledge, there is no shortage ofpeople who write about financial matters. They aren't on the same level as Warren Buffet, or other financial wizards, but they are excellent for *general* advice for someone starting out who isn't managing a huge portfolio or large sums. Your financial education will be ongoing.

One more thing about investing and trusting people: Friends, relatives, co-workers — whoever — may recommend certain investors to you with the promise of handsome returns. *Be careful.* There is a person who was given a prison term of one hundred fifty years for bilking *billions* from too many people, *including charitable foundations,* to fund an enormously extravagant lifestyle. People sang his praises for years until he came clean and confessed to the biggest Ponzi scheme in history. You should be careful enough never to lose even a single dollar to someone like this. So what does being careful entail? It begins and ends with the adage "If it sounds too good to be true, it probably is."

I think it is fair to say that nobody can promise you an extraordinary return from any *legal* investment scheme. Of course, Treasury notes are backed by the government and the returns, while guaranteed, are not out of this world. Banks can offer you a return (presently it's a fraction of a percent) and they are backed by the FDIC. What I'm cautioning you about are the "limited time offer — just invest $1000 or so" that proliferate the world of finance. Good investments sometimes have to be made sooner rather than later, but pressure from someone to "…invest *today* because this is an opportunity to get in at the *ground floor*" can sometimes take you straight to the basement.

Although retirement is a tiny dot in the future for you, and although it may seem premature to think about it, most financial planners will tell you to start saving for that day *NOW.* Besides a 401k, you will be fortunate if your company has a pension plan where you become vested after 5 or 10 years. The monies funding a pension come from the company; when you're completely vested in a pension, you get to keep the money if you leave before you're eligible for retirement. Unfortunately, pensions are quickly becoming a thing of the past. I don't know why, but I hypothesize that it's easier for a company to give money to upper management than distribute it to their employees.

Chapter 13
Spending the Company's Money

Depending on your job, you may dine with current or potential clients. Perhaps your manager will take you and your colleagues to a fancy restaurant to celebrate a milestone or launch of a product. You may attend an out-of-town sales meeting or conference, or during the course of interviewing for a job, a prospective employer may take you out to dinner.

A few tips on dining:

- Should you go to an establishment that provides several pieces of silverware, remember to use them from the outside in

- After you are seated and the waiter brings bread and butter, put your napkin on your lap and use it occasionally throughout the meal, especially if you have a beard or mustache.

- Be very polite to the wait staff, never demanding or condescending.

- Eat slowly, with your mouth closed.

- The plate for your bread roll is on your left. Take a gob of butter and put it on your bread plate. Then rip off a piece of your roll, butter the smaller piece and bite off a chunk to eat. Repeat periodically throughout the meal.

- If you absolutely have to pick your teeth, excuse yourself and go to the restroom.

- If all else fails, watch what your dining partners are doing.

- If a client or company is taking you to dinner and you are the first to order, select a moderately priced meal. Extravagance, even if encouraged by whoever is footing the bill, isn't considerate.

- Don't use alcohol as a crutch to get through the evening. Getting inebriated with colleagues or clients is an efficient way of establishing an unfavorable reputation.
- Refuse alcoholic beverages at lunchtime meetings.

Don't be afraid of some periods of silence during the meal. For people who are still getting to know each other, it's common to have some lapses in the conversation. Even with colleagues you know well, there can be lulls in the usual bantering. To keep the conversation going remember that generally people like to talk about themselves. Try to pick up on the little cues people display: A necktie with a sailboat design, a college alumni sticker on their car window, or an "I'd rather be golfing" bumper sticker. Avoid the other extreme of chattering endlessly. Relax and let the evening evolve as it may. Some people love to talk about their children's accomplishments — or how disappointed they are in them.

Even with video conferencing, traveling for business is still necessary. Meeting and shaking hands with your client or vendor, seeing their manufacturing line, presenting your or your company's ideas, having lunch or dinner together, all contribute to connecting with them on a deeper, more personal level. After meeting them, when you speak to them on the telephone they are more than a voice with a name. It's actually more effective, sometimes, to just fly out there and see how they do it and talk across the table rather than swap phone calls. Sometimes you discover that they don't know what they are doing. And sometimes you gain a whole new respect for people and they see you in a different light.

If you travel for your job

- Use a company credit card wisely. A former boss of mine had what I consider the ideal approach when traveling for the company. He wanted his life while traveling for work to be like his home life. He didn't eat at five star restaurants or fast-food places at home, so he didn't when on the company's dollar. Nor did he drink fine wine with dinner at home so he didn't when out of town on business. He never forgot to call home to check on his family, and he never tried to claim a receipt from a "Gentlemen's Club" was for a business lunch.

- Assuming that you're responsible with money, treat the company's dollar like your own. You are there to accomplish something that will profit your company and you should spend what you need to attain that goal.

- Pay no attention to others' extravagance.

- You have to itemize what you spent in order to get reimbursed for any out-of-pocket expenses, so request a receipt for everything, including tolls and parking.

Chapter 14
Presentations and Meetings

It is critical to know the essentials of a good meeting,
and how to prepare and deliver a presentation.

I've thrown in a few personal anecdotes for instructional purposes.

I think the common denominator of all companies is the concept of meetings during which you and your colleagues gather to discuss and share information, perhaps as a presentation in which one person is doing the talking.

I have attended countless meetings, as well as listened to and delivered my share of presentations. Most presenters are nervous. This subsides with practice, yet some nervousness is beneficial — it keeps you sharp, on edge, and alert.

Perhaps you should also know that I'm a controlled stutterer. This means that I stutter, but am able to avoid or minimize "blocks", as they're called, by employing a variety of techniques. Stuttering is a neurophysiological problem which ebbs and flows with many factors, some known, some unknown. I have never used it as an excuse; I passed several oral exams in graduate school, defended my master's thesis, haven't shied from any presentation assigned to me, and have never avoided speaking to anyone, anywhere. Even though I've been successful in my career, I'm always a little concerned about the fluidity of my speech in my presentations. It's always there in the dark corners of my consciousness. I feel a special kinship for anyone with an issue of this sort.

Sometimes a meeting will have a "round the table discussion" in which everyone reports on their progress, offers creative excuses for their lack of progress, and hash out their secret agendas. If a manager's meetings are too lean, or they don't have much to report on, they frequently request that their subordinates talk about their projects in order to foster better communication and give more "junior" members some exposure. If you don't want to speak, look away and try to not make eye contact with him if he asking for volunteers, but don't be surprised if your name is called, since he has already given this some thought. One of my earlier managers asked me to give a talk on my project independent of my boss. It was a disaster and I share this so your presentations go a little smoother.

I have to preface this story by stating that I have worked with some extremely pompous, arrogant know-it-alls. Unfortunately, one of them was my boss at the time. I prepared a talk with some slides and discussed my presentation with my boss. He didn't help that much, in fact he confused me more. The data I had were confusing enough, but he added his own thoughts which piled on another level of complexity. Show time arrived, and I took my place in front of the room and began. Halfway into my second sentence, the boss butted in and rephrased what I said. Midway into my first slide he added something I was planning on saying in the next few minutes. And so it went for the longest forty-five minutes of my life. It ended with polite applause. My friends had sympathy for me. A senior member of the group said it was a good talk, which made me understand how cheap (his) compliments can be, because *it wasn't a* good talk. Although I was just annoyed, I felt like a ventriloquist's dummy. True, I wasn't an experienced orator—and my boss *was* an intelligent man and a good speaker—but he should have let me stand on my own two feet and save his comments for the end and offer them to the audience by saying "I would like to add a few points to what Frank said." And if I did do a terrible job, he should have spoken to me about it later on, and offered suggestions for improvement. Sometimes boss and subordinate use a "tag-team" approach to give a presentation, akin to TV news anchors, but in this instance I was the only one on the playbill. He butted in like an overachieving understudy.

So the take-away message here is that to avoid a situation like this, it's a good idea to clarify your boss's tactics if he is going to be in the audience when you are speaking about some activity he is in charge of or involved with. If you perceive him to be hard-headed, come out and request that he either share the stage with you (the tag-team approach) or refrain from corrections and/or interrupting you until you are finished, or at a break in your presentation. For example, when you've finished talking about a point, you can ask your boss if he "has anything to add at this point." If he drones on, you can, when he takes a breath, say something like "I do have more material to cover so perhaps [boss] can present this later." Don't stress out, because you'll have plenty of chances to speak at your job. Put it in perspective: you're not auditioning for the lead in a Broadway play or a delivering a valedictory speech. You have to build up some credibility before your boss puts you out front, but sooner or later, you should be encouraged to deliver your message alone.

There was an event at another presentation that I didn't handle correctly, except my boss (a different boss from the previous story) was the *speaker* and I was in the audience. This boss was also a leader in the pompous-arrogant-know-it-all category.

I had just started working with this fellow. Our task was to continue some work a former boss and I had initiated. He was presenting a review of our work and his plans for future work.

About ten minutes into his talk he began telling the audience of about 50 people how incorrect my former boss and I were in our approach, how we didn't do this and that, we didn't know what we were doing and so on. I sat there, embarrassed, angry, and perplexed. I wondered if I was being pranked for a hidden camera comedy special. Here was my new boss essentially ridiculing my work in front of all of these people. Was he correct? No, absolutely not. I'm sure we made some mistakes, but we didn't make any outrageous claims or violate any laws of nature. We had sound arguments and data to back it up. My new boss eventually agreed, privately, many, many months later, with the conclusions we made, but he didn't announce it in a meeting. There was considerable rivalry between the two bosses which might have fueled the new one's unprofessional tirade. I let it slide, pretended that it didn't happen, and worked hard for the new guy. After about 1½ years, I found another project and moved on. There was no harm done to my career, as I was too deep in the trenches to be affected. But how I handled this was completely wrong. I should have

- Spoken privately to our mutual manager, and his manager, and recounted how my new boss ridiculed and attempted to discredit my work.

- Insisted that new boss distribute a written apology to all attendees.

- Insisted on an immediate transfer to a different project.

The take away message here is to never let assaults on your character go uncorrected and never attack someone's credibility or work. If you disagree with someone's method or conclusions and they intertwine with your message in a presentation:

- Speak to them beforehand and tell them of the conflict

- Low-ball any criticisms you are forced to make. You can try dancing around the issue, but the audience will realize (or already know) of the problem.

- If you're backed into a corner, state the conflict in polite terms, mention that it is unresolved, assure them that a resolution will be forthcoming, and move on.

- Never, ever, air your grievances pertaining to your work on social media! Once you publish anything on any aspect of the internet, rest assured that it is there forever!

Presentations at work will not be a problem as long as you have a true story to tell and you tell it so that people can understand it. The story needs facts to support it and facts come from data or designs or more generally, output from you and your workgroup. If you haven't been doing anything, then you're screwed, but you deserve it. If you have something to present that is controversial be prepared to defend what you're presenting. Tell the truth, present the facts, and if they don't believe you, keep telling them until someone can show you otherwise. Remember that when presenting, form follows function. Snazzy slides with sound effects and acrobatics won't improve a bad story. Present on what you're supposed to, and be complete and concise: No one except your mother wants to hear your voice that much.

Preparation is the key for any presentation.

Work with your boss on your first presentation. Go into his office with slides you prepared on what you think your presentation should look like, show them to him, and listen to what he says. It's a given that he'll have some worthwhile input.

A basic rule of thumb for presentations is to

- Tell them what you're going to tell them — an outline.
- Tell them, or deliver your presentation.
- Tell them what you told them. Review what you just covered.

Begin preparing for a presentation well before the date it is due. A boss of mine used to paraphrase what is printed on the side mirrors on cars: "...deadlines (or dates for presentations) are closer than they appear."

More than likely you'll be using Microsoft PowerPoint for your presentation. Form follows function, not the other way around. The opportunity to razzle-dazzle your audience is tempting, but don't give in!

- Select a font that is easy to read
- Present the facts clearly; don't overload a slide with too many messages
- Keep in mind that the audience wants a "take-away message." It's a nice way of saying "remember this" or condensing the main message from a slide. Your presentation can have many take-away messages, which lend themselves to a summary slide.
- On a separate slide, give credit by name to everyone involved, whatever their contribution.
- It is wise to prepare back-up slides containing information with greater depth on topics someone might ask about.
- Relish the endorphins flooding your system after you've completed your talk.

If you're asked a question you truly don't know the answer to, DO NOT even THINK of improvising (bullshitting) your answer. Remember you're not a contestant on a question-and-answer game show, so you *can* say you "have to think about that for a bit." Don't say "I don't know" and leave it like that. You might be able to say *something* about the question, such as that it is a very good question (not to compliment them, but acknowledge their thoughts) or offer a partial thought. You can also invite someone whom you believe knows the answer to comment. Rephrasing the question and repeating it back to the asker, or asking for clarification is a common stall tactic, but can also reinforce that you understand what the question is. Either way, if you're stuck out there by yourself, always tell the truth: if you don't know, ask "Can I get back to you on that question?" as a nice evasive way of saying that you don't know. Sometimes the answer to the puzzling question may come to you later in your presentation. You can always find some way to bring the topic up (before you forget it again) or speak to person who posed the question after you've completed your talk.

Elements of a good meeting

Every meeting, even if you're just meeting with a couple of your colleagues, requires a clear agenda. The agenda is usually prepared by the person who called or who is in charge of the meeting. It doesn't have to be lengthy with time allocated down to the minute, but at least cover the main topic(s). If more than one person is going to speak, it should list who is speaking on what topic or action item (assigned task) and the approximate time allotted to them. The agenda itself can be on the agenda, in case someone wants to include other topics. If you or someone else wants to know about a topic that wasn't scheduled to be discussed, the best time to bring it up is when the agenda is presented. Maybe someone else will be talking about that in yet another meeting, or it was omitted from the current meeting in error. Either way, at least you and everyone else will know. At the end of the agenda, there should time provided for questions and answers or feedback or discussion. The audience always wants to be able to offer their suggestions or comments.

Following a review of the agenda, the meeting is under way with someone in the limelight. Pay attention—and don't look to me as a role model here. I shamefully admit that unless I care deeply about the subject, a speaker has about five minutes to get and maintain my attention. Should I deem the material uninteresting or the presenter monotonous in his delivery, I begin to enter an altered state of consciousness—neither asleep nor fully aware. As I mentioned in an earlier chapter, three minutes at big-picture meetings with vice presidents are equivalent to two sleeping pills. And to boot, I am powerless to do anything about it. I've have stuck myself with my mechanical pencil when Mr. Sandman seems to be at the door, stood against the wall—you name it. Clearly, this is not the way to be. I'm not alone by any means—you will see many bored colleagues throughout your career. I take most of the blame, but admit that dull presenters contribute to some degree.

Meetings can proceed smoothly according to the agenda, or they can be dysfunctional wastes of time. If you're in charge or an attendee, I offer you the following suggestions:

- Don't arrive late to a meeting. It's rude and disruptive to both the speaker and audience.
- Don't hold your own side discussion during the meeting. No matter how softly you seem to be speaking, others can still hear you and it's annoying. Both parties should step outside

the room if they need to speak to each other. Nothing is more disruptive than two people having their own private meeting while someone else is speaking. If someone tries to engage you in a whispered side chat, you can whisper back for them to wait until after the meeting or resort to passing notes like in grammar school. In most cases, *nothing* is so important that it can't wait. A colleague of mine would loudly retort "One meeting, everyone, one meeting please!" when two people starting chatting.

In one of my workgroups, our leader would hold court (at *lunchtime,* for goodness sake) and adapted the Native American custom of a "talking piece", which I believe was a pot or jug or something that only the person speaking would hold. No talking piece, no talking. Unfortunately our talking piece was the shaft of a golf club with the head missing. Let me caution you: while we never experienced any bloodshed, a rigid metal shaft with a moderately pointed end is not a suitable talking piece. A football, okay. A soft rubber ball, okay. A baseball bat, NO, nothing that can inflict bodily harm. Sometimes one person would be talking and, to involve someone else in the group, they would extend the shaft over the table so the other person could hold the free end and be granted permission to speak! Believe me, this workgroup was as dysfunctional as it sounds.

Leave your annoying mannerisms elsewhere. I worked with a fellow who was constantly jingling his car keys or loose coins in his pocket. He would be in a meeting or presenting something and his hand would be going like mad in his pocket. I've never been able to shut out noises that I deem distracting so it drove me nuts. Here I am, trying to act like I care about what is going on and this goon needs to make distracting noises. Lucky for me, this fellow wasn't a regular presence at our meetings. Snapping gum, however, is something that no one gets away with. It's annoying to the human race and probably to some advanced primates, too. This is one issue that has to be confronted head on.

Additional thoughts for successful meetings

Stay on topic. An important topic may have been overlooked, but let whoever is in charge of the meeting decide to either fit it into the agenda or discuss it at another meeting.

Brevity is a virtue. I would hope that I'm not describing you, but for heaven's sake, don't fall in love with the sound of your own voice. There are many facets to every problem or discussion, but you don't have to cover all of them. Don't monopolize the meeting.

Don't interrupt. When someone else is speaking, hold your thought until they are done. Maybe what he's said is outrageous but let him finish and don't tailgate onto the period of his sentence.

Leave personal vendettas at the door. I recounted earlier how a former boss of mine attempted to discredit work an earlier boss and I had done. Don't use a meeting to grind your axes.

Put your cell phone on vibrate and don't even *think* of answering it in the conference room. If you're expecting an important call (relative who's ill, pregnant wife, etc.), sit close to the door to make a quick escape when you feel your phone vibrate.

Ask for feedback. If your meeting wasn't as productive as you hoped for, or your presentation didn't flow like you had planned, understand that you are on a learning curve. Hosting meetings and giving presentations is an acquired talent or skill. Practice makes for improvements.

- I attended many meetings held by a fellow who spoke with his hand over his mouth. He also tended to mumble, so the combination of the two habits made him nearly incomprehensible.

- Ask questions if you are confused. This may seem obvious, but many people do not want to appear ignorant so they sit there and become increasingly befuddled.

- Conclude your meeting with a summary slide

One of the duties of hosting or facilitating the meeting is that you may be responsible for delegating what has to done if there is a follow-up meeting. These things to do are referred to as "action items." Everyone's goal is not to be assigned too many action items, or for them to be relatively easy if they can't avoid them. If you have action items, you will be required to report on their status at the beginning of the following meeting. If you have to speak briefly at a meeting, aim for presenting towards the end of the meeting. By that time, everyone is getting antsy and wants to do something else, and may not want to debate or challenge any controversial points you make. Or they may delay your contribution until the next meeting, so you have extra time to fine-tune what you have to say.

If you have to deliver a presentation, try to schedule it for eleven in the morning. People might have plans for lunch at twelve or just be getting hungry, so they will not be inclined to debate what you have presented. People who ask many questions will be given dirty looks by the attendees who want to leave which may suggest that the grand inquisitor continue on his own time. I owe this tip to my graduate thesis advisor's *wife* who suggested it to me. And it works, too.

Generating gibberish for reports and presentations

Philip Broughton was an official with the U.S. Public Health Service when, in 1968, he popularized what he called the "Systematic Buzz

Phrase Projector." The system uses only thirty words, shown in the following table:

0 Integrated	0 Management	0 Options
1 Total	1 Organizational	1 Flexibility
2 Systematized	2 Monitored	2 Capability
3 Parallel	3 Reciprocal	3 Mobility
4 Functional	4 Digital	4 Programming
5 Responsive	5 Logistical	5 Concept
6 Optional	6 Transitional	6 Time-phase
7 Synchronized	7 Incremental	7 Projection
8 Compatible	8 Third-generation	8 Hardware
9 Balanced	9 Policy	9 Contingency

To use Broughton's chart, just think of any three digit number and pick the corresponding words from each column. The number 153 gives "total logistical mobility" which sounds perfect for . . . who knows what? Similarly, 217 translates to "systemized organizational projection" which will undoubtedly make you sound like an absolute genius!

Mr. Broughton was obviously fed up with buzz words and gobbledygook tech speak that he heard in meetings and read in reports, and supposedly said that "Nobody will have the remotest idea what you're talking about, but the most important thing is that no one is about to admit it."

Pay close attention to what you hear in meetings and read in reports—some of it may sound very close to what is in Broughton's chart.

Chapter 15
The Miracle of Teamwork and Nurturing Your Ideas

I would be remiss as a technical guy if I didn't include a chapter on what to do when the light bulb in your head begins to glow. It's in my blood: I'm a co-author of many U.S. patents and have been curious, creative and innovative since I was a boy.

As enticing as it can be, don't fall blindly in love with your ideas. If you remain closed to change, improvements, or refinements from others, you are forgoing the opportunity to turn a mediocre idea into a *fantastic* idea. By itself, the human mind is amazing; two or more human minds working together can be astounding. A synergism can develop when more than one mind works on a problem. The first person will suggest something; the second will counter it or perhaps find an error in the suggestion, and counter-suggest something. From those words, the first person may suddenly gain new insight into the cause and solution to the problem and have even more new ideas or efficient ways to tackle the issue being discussed. It's really amazing when you see it happen and it's a great rush when you're involved in the process. You never know when your brain will be stimulated to a higher level of understanding. Sometimes you have to let go of the idea or problem and then when you're washing your car or doing some unrelated activity—

WHAM!—the solution hits you right between the eyes. It's kind of what happens when you are unsuccessfully tearing the house apart to find something, yet it remains hidden until days later when you're not looking for it, and then you almost trip over it. Ideas, solutions to problems—whatever—are in many instances discovered in the same manner. The point here is not to give up thinking. So you have an idea that you think has a lot of potential and you're proud of and consequently discover that it's not feasible for some reason. Don't become discouraged! There's another idea in the pipes that will surface.

There are plenty of problems and opportunities for innovation in every facet of a company. The only item missing is the willingness of people to conceive and suggest a solution. Some people don't care and don't want to—all they are concerned about is completing their assigned tasks and going home. They may feel that the company isn't entitled to their thoughts, or that they aren't paid enough to solve the company's problems. They're entitled to their feelings. Other people can have ideas to share but for one reason or another are hesitant to suggest anything. Maybe, for example, they're a pipefitter with the building facilities department and doesn't see an outlet for his idea or his supervisor doesn't encourage thinking outside the box. There's not a simple solution for people in these two groups. Their main goal should be to find someone to listen to the idea. Some companies have formal suggestion programs, but these require manpower and infrastructure to be worthwhile, which do not mix well with cost-cutting measures that seemingly every company is undertaking.

In an industrial research and development organization and in academia, where fundamental research may be done under contract to companies or independently by students and their professors, there is something called *intellectual property*. In broad strokes, this takes the form of inventions, good ideas and trade secrets, that people in the organization developed or discovered, which enable the company (or some individual) to do something profitable or *prevents competitors* from doing something profitable. Most companies claim ownership of any inventions or discoveries of their employees. Depending on upon your job and where in the company you work, you might sign a form on your first day that gives the company all the rights to whatever you invent in the course of doing your job. And they deserve the rights, too, since you're using *their* laboratories, *their* equipment which *they* purchased with *their* money and paid decent money to you to come up with good ideas. They encounter a lot of other expenses, such as the patent lawyers, who are not known for working cheaply, and exorbitant fees to the U.S. or foreign patent offices for *their* expensive lawyers.

Where I worked for the majority of my career, there were specific procedures for inventions. You had to first compile it into a document in which you covered the concept, utility, advantages and limitations, and any earlier work done on similar ideas. The disclosure had to pass through many gates where it may have been deemed patentable or perhaps an interesting idea that should remain an undisclosed internal process. This required lots of people, including a slew of patent attorneys. Most patents included more than one person. When you were the principle author (your name is first) of an idea that was deemed patentable, you had to do plenty of time-consuming work with the attorney. In the end, when a patent was applied for, you received $300 (minus taxes, of course). A very few prolific inventors (or prolific at getting their name on an invention disclosure) had well over one hundred fifty patents. Do the math. In addition to the financial awards, there is the prestige of having over one hundred patents. Suddenly you're viewed with greater distinction and consulted with on other individuals' ideas, which may get you on more patents, and so on.

While I will stop short of calling it a game, let's just say there some lesser-known suggestions for getting a new idea accepted in a company. The most helpful is an ombudsman, mentor, or more appropriately, *godfather* for your idea. The higher status this person has in the organization, the better. And it helps if his name is on the invention, though not first author since the idea didn't originate with him. The gatekeepers of the invention process believe that when a senior person endorses someone else's idea several points in the credibility department are accumulated. The reason for this is that the senior person will likely offer (or even mandate) suggestions or clarifications. His or her experience is invaluable, and if you are intelligent enough to accept their advice, you get a free lesson!

Companies can hold *brainstorming* sessions to seed a group's creative process for solving a current problem or issue. This process can be applied to either a technical or a non-technical group. These sessions are usually run by a facilitator who keeps everyone in line and generally keeps the process going. People usually sit around a table and take turns suggesting solutions to the problem. The facilitator can also act as a scribe to document the ideas. The rules are few, but include not criticizing or judging anyone else's idea, no matter how far-fetched or inconceivable it may appear to be. Brainstorming sessions serve as a breeding ground for solutions to many types of problems, and capitalize on the teamwork approach I mentioned at the start of this chapter.

If you have an idea for something that isn't in your organization's line of business and you want to patent it (at your expense), you can ask your company to allow you to do so. Just make sure it's worth your while. Bounce the idea off someone you trust, or go schedule a meeting with a patent attorney not affiliated with your company.

Stay far away from—or at least thoroughly investigate— companies that offer their services to market your idea or claim that they are in desperate need of inventions. They will likely be thrilled with your idea and will encourage you to proceed to the next stage of their process where they perform a "money-ectomy" on your personal savings.

Be sure to record all of your ideas in a notebook, and include the names of anyone who provided assistance to you, especially for work-related ideas. Leave it alone for a day or so and then come back to it. Read it again, and add anything you've thought of that clarifies it. Add whatever you can think of or find in terms of drawings, facts, examples, justifications, business value, market share, or related ideas and devices. If you have an idea that isn't mainstream and may be construed as foolish, write that down too in your personal (not company issued) notebook. The point here is to keep track of what you've been thinking so you do not forget that great idea.

Chapter 16
When Love is in the Air

I know how it happens — a mind-numbing meeting, a glance across the conference room at the attractive person with the nice smile. Suddenly, you're seeing this person everywhere — the cafeteria, the coffee club, and when you pass in the hall, you smile. The next time you offer a smile and demure "Hi." The third finger on his/her left hand says "Maybe available." You might catch the him/her looking your way at the next project meeting so you begin planning your approach.

"Don't get your meat the same place you get your bread" is a succinct but somewhat unrefined way of looking at the situation.

If you are contemplating an office romance, keep in mind that the *last* thing you need is to go to work and have any kind of possible conflict with a person you are in a romantic relationship with. Hurt feelings, misunderstandings, one-sided attraction, a paternity suit – you name it – all of them would contribute to your distraction and could make your life a living hell. There's no need for me to play out the scenarios for you, but your love interest and/or injured party can make it very difficult for you to continue in the same manner as before you showed an interest in them. And how will you feel if this person takes up with someone else?

If you *have* to connect with this person, a safe approach is to invite him/her to join you for lunch in the company cafeteria or out with friends you've made at work. You get to observe this person outside of work, pick up on any signals, see what he/she laugh at and interests they have, and converse. You'll test the waters, so to speak and nurture the friendship. If he/she brings someone and it appears that they are a couple, you may decide to not pursue the relationship any further.

There is one iron-clad rule with office admirations and romances: No means NO.

It doesn't mean maybe; it's *no, negative, not, never.* If you decide to ask this person out and he/she refuses, smile and make your exit. Don't ask him/her again and whatever you do, don't hover or do anything that could be construed as *stalking,* unless, of course, you want to lose your job. I have seen this happen on more than one occasion. Unwanted attention is taken very seriously, as it should be. I'm not advising you to reverse your direction if you're headed towards each other in the hallway; after all, you both work in the same place and are bound to encounter each other from time to time. Just don't *happen* to be in the same place as he or she is *all the time.* If you pass him/her in the hall, smile and say "Hi." In my bachelor years I did, on a few occasions, get my nerve up and attempt to initiate a friendship with women I worked with. While I'm still friends with them, there wasn't any conflict because I was alert to the, uh, "lack of encouragement" I received.

I think for both men and women, it's important to be kind, be open, listen, be friendly, and let yourself mature in the workplace. In time, you will find out who you can be friends with. Be careful what details about your life you share. You don't need the stress (in the form of gossip) about a failed intimate romance. I've also known of affairs between consenting employees. Sometimes a marriage results, sometimes not, but to be sure reputations of all involved get "discussed". In spite of how secretive they may be, people *will* find out and *will* talk about it. Some people are overly impressed with executives and covet their attention. They are just people in nice clothes who work a lot and make much more money than you. Don't be impressed by what you perceive as their powerful status in the company. It's their integrity that matters, not their power.

If you and a colleague want to start a serious relationship, go slowly. If the man or woman is married, STAY CLEAR. If he/she laments that their wife or husband doesn't understand him/her, your response should be that you "hope things work out and that you find peace in your life." Run fast, run far, and don't look back.

Chapter 17
If You're Working in Customer Service

We are all working in customer service—everyone who has a job, has a customer. And if you have customers, you have to fulfill their requirements. For some, it's their immediate supervisor and for others, it can be an irate person seeking clarification on their account, a confused user of some software, or innumerable people with innumerable problems.

It is essential for you to identify who your customers are and what they want from you. I've spoken about many facets of this in earlier chapters. I'm speaking now primarily to those dealing with the public: wait staff, front desk people, cashiers, clerks, call center representatives, and so on. To begin with,

- You are not doing your customers a favor by doing your job, so don't expect them to thank you. They probably will, though.

- You should thank the customers because the money is coming from their pockets to your cash drawer.

- You will become frustrated in your dealings with people and feel the need to vent. Social media is not the place to detail your interaction with the impatient customer, the patron who didn't leave any gratuity, or the smelly person who wore a striped shirt with plaid trousers and talked to himself.

Some, or even many of your customers will thank you because you helped them settle a problem with their account, repaired their vehicle, served them a meal, fixed their computer, sold them shoes, or rang up their groceries—whatever. You provided them with excellent customer service, which they paid your employer for, and they are appreciative.

- Your response to their "Thank you" *is not* "No problem", "Yup", "No sweat", or anything else like that.

- There is but one correct response, and that is "You are welcome" and it's delivered sincerely and with a smile.

- Refrain from addressing a group of people as "you guys", even if all the people you're serving are male. Consider saying "Good afternoon, everyone" or Good evening, folks" as an alternative. Groups of just men or just women should be addressed as gentlemen or ladies.

- Consider moving closer to the most elderly person when taking orders or describing menu items. Chances are that he or she has some difficulty hearing and shouting today's specials at them from across the table isn't correct.

- Speaking louder to someone who is hard of hearing doesn't necessarily make anything easier to understand, but only serves to garble the words for them even more.

- Even though you've be asked what salad dressings are available, or described the trout almondine, seventy-five times today, remember to *slow down* when you're asked the seventy-sixth time. Rattling through it, especially with elderly clientele, only confuses them, conveys impatience, and makes them ask again, and again, and again. . .

- Be kind to the elderly because believe it or not, you'll get there someday.

- People who are profoundly hard of hearing can be amazingly proficient at reading lips but you must speak directly to them so they can see your lips move.

Customer service is difficult because people are unpredictable. While most people are kind, friendly, clear-headed and reasonable, there are countless others who are unreasonable, rude, condescending, mean, impatient, dense, angry, irrational, and indecisive, to name a few. Unfortunately, you never know what kind of person you will be dealing with, so you should always start out on the high road. As a young man, I worked in retail electronics sales and I understand how crazy some people can be. I also realized that for some reason, I always found it easy to remember the difficult people rather than the "good" customers. Try to focus on the customers who have been reasonable and a pleasure to deal with, and resolve to not let the others ruin your attitude. Remember, you give them power when they affect you.

On numerous occasions, I've heard that my call to customer service "may be monitored for quality and training purposes." This is a good thing, too, as everyone else's work is monitored for the same reasons. Why should the people who work at call centers be exempt? I think a lot of us, at times, take these people for granted and take out our frustrations and resentment—about service glitches, account errors, and increases in the price of cable, cell phone, or internet service—on the people that happen to take our call. It's wrong, of course, or at the minimum, not nice. In the past, I've succumbed to losing my patience and am now determined not to be angry, but to stay on the line, calmly explain as many times as necessary until I feel the representative has completely understood and resolved my problem, and then sincerely thank the representative for his/her help. I usually get what I want.

For the dedicated, patient souls who take these calls, continue to greet and treat each new call as if you are speaking to a dear friend. I prescribe regular exercise to cope with the stress, along with remembering that when you complete a call with a difficult person, it's over. That person is gone—imagine that when the call ends, their negativity is retracted from your headset back to their location.

Afterword

I struggle to find a final message for you at this point. While many of the situations that I've shared with you have a disagreeable flavor to them, it is not my intent to portray the working world as a step into a lower level of *Dante's Inferno*. I think that an effective method of learning is from the experiences of others. Perhaps that's how apprenticeships began—what better way to learn a skill than by working closely with someone much more experienced who has made his share of mistakes and learned the correct way to do things. Perhaps the master of the trade may tell the apprentice not to approach a task in a certain manner because, from his firsthand experience, he knows that it will not yield the expected result or may even cause injury. And sometimes the master has to let the apprentice make mistakes in order for him to learn from them.

When I'm on vacation, I miss, next to family members not with me, my friends from work. It may just be the type of person I am, but I care about everyone I work with, even if I get annoyed with a few of them at times. A smile or friendly greeting from a co-worker can give you a much needed lift on a day at work.

Here's one final quote from H. Jackson Browne. I offer it to you with my utmost sincerity for an enjoyable, successful, and productive career.

"Twenty years from now you will be more disappointed by the things that you didn't do than by the ones you did do. So throw off the bowlines. Sail away from the safe harbor. Catch the trade winds in your sails. Explore. Dream. Discover."

Life, my friends, is incredibly short. While you may occasionally wonder if time has stood still, your tenure in the workplace will accumulate faster than you think. You will grow older, your family will grow, you will have successes, setbacks, joys and sorrows. Life is not a dress rehearsal so I implore you *not* to put off experiencing the joys of living until you are older because sadly, not everyone is given the same length of lifetime. Take that trip, smell those flowers, show love to your family and friends, and be kind.

If you wish to contact the author to share a story, comments, or any other reason, he can be reached at unclefranksguide@gmail.com

Acknowledgements

I was fortunate to have the assistance of many individuals in the production of Uncle Frank's Guide.

I met Mary Beth Egeling at her workshop on Self-Publishing. Actually, that is not entirely correct. Mary Beth was selling her instruments from her former career as a dental hygienist on Craigslist; when I arrived at her home to pick up some of those picks and probes for my workshop, I realized it was once owned by my aunt and uncle. Warm, friendly, and welcoming Mary Beth and I began to chat, and I shared my efforts over writing this book. That's when she told me about her workshops on self-publishing which I subsequently attended. As an author of several books, she proofread drafts of mine and is my trusted friend, advisor, mentor, and critic. Without her, this book would not have been realized.

I became acquainted with Dorie Jennings during my search on LinkedIn for a grammar and punctuation proofreader of my next-to-final draft. I also wanted another opinion on what I had written. Dorie was most wonderful to work with! Besides correcting my grammar, shared her thoughts on several sections of the book, which I was fortunately smart enough to accept. Her enthusiasm for my ideas buoyed me during some of the darker days of writing.

I also met Sheila Kennedy during my LinkedIn search. As an author of several books and editor of many more, Sheila gave generously of her time and knowledge to advise and encourage me and point me towards Rich Selby; the man responsible for printing this book. I felt at ease with Rich Selby the first time I spoke with him. I appreciate and admire his willingness to answer my many questions. I was anxious about working with a printer, but Rich's friendly nature and guidance allayed my concerns.

I've known Debra Atkins-Manos since, uh . . . maybe I shouldn't give dates. But her husband, then boyfriend, John, and I were chemistry students at Rochester Institute of Technology. Over the years, we've danced at each other's wedding and when our schedules allowed, got together with our spouses for an evening of friendship and laughter. Deb's expertise as a graphics designer is unparalleled. I always knew she was good at what does, but it wasn't before she agreed to work with me on this project did I realize how fortunate I am to know her and have her extensive experience and expertise on formatting and design available to me. I looked forward to seeing Deb, as we laughed, sipped coffee, updated each other on our families and friends, and honed the final pages you will be reading.

Throughout this project, my wife Barbara has been an indefatigable supporter of my efforts. Our discussions on many topics were invaluable but her love and encouragement sustained me throughout the journey. Behind every author, there must be a loving and understanding spouse.

Made in the USA
Middletown, DE
01 February 2020

84032562R00113